P9-AQH-427

THE YANKEE TRIVIA BOOK

THE
YANKEE TRIVIA
BOOK

Peter Farrow

LANCE TAPLEY, PUBLISHER

©1985 by Peter Farrow. All rights reserved.

No part of this book may be reproduced or transmitted in any form or by any means, electronic or mechanical, including photocopying, recording, or by any information storage and retrieval system, without the written permission of the publisher, except by a reviewer quoting brief passages in a magazine, newspaper or broadcast. Address inquiries to Lance Tapley, Publisher, P.O. Box 2439, Augusta, Maine 04330.

Printed in the United States of America.

Library of Congress Cataloging-in-Publication Data

Farrow, Peter.   The Yankee trivia book.

  1. New England — History — Anecdotes, facetiae, satire, etc. 2. New England — Social life and customs — Anecdotes, facetiae, satire, etc. 3. Questions and answers. I. Title.
F4.6.F36 1985 974'.0076 85-14782
ISBN 0-912769-03-3

In remembrance of
JOSHUA DODGE
&
D.P.F.

Contents

PREFACE

I claim for New England Yankees not only the invention of trivia but its perfection.

Locked in by endless winter evenings that huddled a whole family in a cabin's one warm corner, games were as necessary to Yankee survival as food itself — and often scarcer. The Puritan Ethic had banished all the old fireside standbys. Playing cards were fifty-two tickets straight to Hell, chess the Devil's familiar, tic-tac-toe a sin of wastrelry. Even noddy old draughts (which we'd call checkers) was but one jump short of the whipping post. In the doomy shadow of stocks and dunking stool, fun got driven underground — and sprouted back up as the verbal game.

Now the verbal game's a fine subversive thing, needing no paraphernalia and leaving no visible traces, not even bad tempers or churlish pouts. So it came to pass that riddles, conundrums and alphabetics flourished; there was even a flurry of limerick and bawdy motto, epigram and epitaph, not to mention certain unholy improvements on Mother Goose.

But it was trivia that truly blossomed, first nurtured by the Bible, next by that bible-and-umpire of all true trivialists, the Almanack.

Trivia's keenest edge, however, was honed by an unexpected hand: the Yankee schoolmarm. My own Missus Powers, who birched me through eight grades of one-roomed, red-bricked wisdom, seized on this Yankee penchant with a zealot's glee. To the traditional spelling bee was added a swarm of quizzes: multiplication tables, rules of parse, even quizzes on that mystic, unpracticed art called Hygiene. As games, not lessons, she paraded kings, discoverers, patriots, pioneers, inventors, authors, villians, heroes, exemplary fools, presidents in their quadrennially perfect ranks, statesmen, and orators. Then there was that delight of small boys, Wars-and-Enemies, each war with its respective battles, generals, dates, outcomes, sometimes even causes. Missus Powers' own pride was The Boundeds — rattling off the neighbors of each state and nation in perfect compass order.

The result was far from trivial. Trivia and jigsaw puzzle pieces in time get fitted together into whole pictures, and what pieces may be missing are promptly supplied by minds which, helped by trivia, have few Boundeds to them.

And so with this book: By it, you'll find yourself fitting together a picture — I believe a real and honest picture — of the forbears (and, to some extent, of the present bearers of the tradition) of that least bounded of all possible people, the Yankee.

PETER FARROW

Fools & Stumpers

Rules of the Game

This book can be used as just a book: read straight through, dipped into for a nibble now and then, then tucked away into your blizzard box against more drastic times. But it's also a game for one or more players — and that, of course, means rules.

A question may sound like a riddle. None is, nor is it a conundrum, requiring a pun or a word play for an answer. Almost all questions have "straight" answers, often amazing but nonetheless true. But please note that we jump around from century to century a bit. That's just to keep you on your toes.

Many questions are marked with one, two or three little stumps. These are *stumpers*, truly tough questions. Each stump is worth an extra point.

Any question, however, can *earn the fool* (good for one point) if all players agree that you've answered so far wrong that you've made up in wit what you lacked in knowledge.

The book is set up in general categories — Weather, Food, Ghosts, Courting, etc. — so you can play by subject, each player picking his or her own subject to ask the others.

You can play straight through, front to back.

Or back to front.

Or skipping around.

You can even play upside down: Give the answer and see who comes up with the question.

If you need more rules, just make 'em up.

1.
Rockribs & Chiselwits
The Yankee Defined

Since this book deals with Yankees, and since Yankees can be pretty tricky critters, before you get yourself in too deep you'd better have some notion of what we're talking about. Here are some that go to the heart of the matter. (These require the least straight answers in the book, however. If you're playing a game, you might want to start the scorekeeping with Chapter 2.)

1. Where does the word *Yankee* come from?

Frankly, the professors are still tussling with this one, but most hold that Yankee came from the Indians' attempt to pronounce *anglais,* the French word for English. One Abenaki Indian I knew said it meant "rude stinker." Its use as a suffix for *damned* is confined to Southerners and overcharged summer complaints.

2. What's the surest way to tell who *isn't* a real Yankee?

Anybody who's rock-ribbed, chisel-witted, grudging in manner, laconic in speech, parsimonious in purse, grunts an *ayuh* to everything and spatters homely old nostrums in all directions wherever he may be...chances are he's no Yankee but just another displaced New Yorker trying to blend into the Good Life — and probably writing a book about it, too.

3. Does Yankee apply equally to all New Englanders?

Ye gods, no! Looking at it from my perch in Maine, I see Yankees in six degrees. In ascending order they are: Massachusetts, Connecticut, Rhode Island, New Hampshire, Vermont and Maine Yankees. While opinions may differ, all agree that Bostonians are not Yankees, just Bostonians — a race apart.

4. What state produces the most *ornery* Yankees?

New Hampshire, of course. "Hated on three sides, despised on the fourth, envied by all — and well worth it," boasted one old Granite Stater. Flagrantly low taxes, cheap cigarettes, cheaper likker, insane presidential primaries and the frustrated career of Dan'l Webster have been contributing causes.

2.

Catspaws & Goosethaws

Yankee Weather

God invented weather, rumor has it, just to give Yankees something to talk about. And talk they do. Weather is always the first and often the only topic of conversation. But the talk's not trivial. Yankees live by the weather —and often in spite of it.

These questions should help you pick up a few pointers no TV weatherman yet knows nor satellite discerns.

1. Should you hold a picnic on a day that's a *weatherbreeder*?

Yes, indeed! A weatherbreeder is a day so clear and fine it *must* be breeding up bad weather. This isn't just Yankee pessimism. A cloudless afternoon in summer almost always means poor weather within two days, usually sooner. And the more weatherbreeders you have in a row, the worse the change will be. Check it out for yourself.

2. What do geese do in a *goosethaw*?

Head north, if they're dumb. Stay south, if they're smart. A goosethaw is a thaw so warm and long it could fool a goose into returning.

3. Is a *green winter* a good thing?

No. "A green winter means a fat churchyard..." goes the old Yankee saying. Warm, open winters seemed to bring on epidemics, deaths and thus well-filled churchyards. Viruses, we now know, along with other germs, get roused up in warm weather and go looking for new living quarters. Added to this is the fact that folks who weren't "bound in" by winter got around more and so spread disease.

4. Is a *green sky* a sign of spring?

No. Absolutely the opposite. A green sky in winter, especially at sundown, means a stretch of bitter cold is about to descend — and likely to stay awhile, too.

5.   Should you be insulted if called a *March fool*?

Yes, but only if you're edgy by nature. A March fool is merely an optimist, someone who'd see signs of spring even in December. Often used as a disclaimer: "I don't want to sound like a March fool, but..."

6.   If you were on a ship and saw a *marestail,* what should you do?

Stand by to shorten sail. A marestail is a very high, thin, wispy cloud formation, foretelling poor weather and high winds. No less ominous than *mackerel scales,* which are lower, thicker clouds mottled like the fish's sides. Thus the old rhyme:

> *"Marestails and mackerel scales*
> *Make tall ships take in their sails."*

Or, as I heard it,

> *"...Make whalermen forsake the whales."*

7.   How did they plow town roads in the old days?

They rolled them. Which is not really plowing. Generally, snow was not considered a Bad Thing. It provided the best chance by far for heavy land transport, not to mention logging and stone-wall building. So public roads were often rolled to form a firm sledding surface. Sometimes, in fact, snow was shovelled *onto* the road to patch up spots gone bare. Covered bridges had to be not plowed, but snowed.

8. When might you get caught in a *line storm*?

If you listen to these new-fangled, college-educated experts on TV, who claim there's no such thing as a line storm, you'd think they didn't exist. But any Yankee knows there are always two each year, at the equinoxes (March 21 and September 21, roughly). That's when the sun "crosses the line" and the days and nights are of equal length. An occasion like that isn't going to slip by without the weather doing something about it. The storm may not fall quite on the exact day, but a line storm you're going to have. (I've heard these two storms called *noxies,* and the March storm called an *Ider.*)

9. What are *dog days*? And when and why?

Every dog will have his day, but a wise one won't pick a *dog day*. These are the hot, sultry, muggy days of late summer when "everything's sticky but nothin' stays stuck." The name comes from no earthly canine but from the Dog Star, Sirius, which at that time of year again makes its appearance. Look for it just before dawn in the sou'east, behind Orion.

10. Do mosquitoes bite more before a rain?

Oh my yes indeed! Sure sign of rain, every time. Needing blood to whip up a batch of eggs, they'll rampage you at the first hint that a puddle might be forthcoming. All other bites are just to keep in practice.

11. When leaves show their bellies, what weather is in store?

Showers and probably thunderstorms. It's caused by a bunch of little winds (thermals) blowing straight up and looking for mischief. A silver maple was often planted by the washyard, where its dazzly underparts could warn the Old Lady to come get the clothes in from the line. One old Vermonter claimed he could end a drought anytime: "I just send Molly out to shake the washyard tree."

12. When would you likely have a *honeycomb*?

Another kind of fine hot day, but in March, with the sun melting the snow so fast it "rots," forming honeycombs of ice. An absolutely, positively, infallibly certain sign of spring. Some years.

13. What is a *sugar snow*?

To a Yankee, sugar snow has nothing to do with a granular frosting on six slopes. Sugar snow is that wet, large-flaked article usually occurring during maple-sugar days in early spring.

14. And what is an *apple snow*?

An apple snow isn't a snow at all, and a perfect one you may see only once in your life — and count yourself lucky at that. (I've seen three, plus a half-dozen also-rans.) It happens when apple blossoms drop their petals at exactly the same time when exactly the right kind of breeze is blowing on exactly the right kind of May night when the moon is exactly full. An apple snow can last ten minutes or several hours. Even a minute's worth is the most magical thing in New England.

15. What's the weather doing when *the Devil beats his wife*?

The Devil is beating his wife when it's raining (or snowing) in full sunshine. What she has to do with it, nobody knows. Probably not even the Devil.

16. When is *Missus Grundy making up the bed*?

You may also hear this as "Mother Grundy's shakin' up the featherbed." It refers to those oversized, lazy, sparse flakes of snow with no serious intention of becoming a storm. If it should turn into a real snowfall, then you may hear, "B'gawd! She must of ripped it *this* time!"

17. What's a *catspaw* and what's it a certain sign of?

A catspaw is a light spanking of wind made visible on the surface of still water, patting it only here and there and leaving no waves behind. It's a sure sign that, back on land, Molly's out hustling in the wash — although they also occur at the end of the day when an offshore wind begins.

3.

Times Arjus,
Teejus & Dubrus

Yankee History, Revised

"When life ain't arjus, it's teejus," remarked one ancient Yankee. "An' either way, it's forever dubrus..." (Times Arjus is also another name for the *Times-Argus*, a Vermont newspaper.)

Sadly, the arduous, tedious and dubious seldom catch the fancy of historians, and the picture of New England's early days that schoolbooks present gets filled up with resolute Pilgrims. The actual, day-after-day Yankee history remains unwritten. Here is a batch of trivia that might lighten the subject up a mite.

1. Did the first Yankees come over on the *Mayflower*?

No. They were already here, and some in their second generation. Seasonal fishing stations — some more or less permanent — existed on the Maine coast at Monhegan and Damariscove long before 1620. It was the folks on Monhegan who saved the Plymouth Colony from starvation during their first winters.

And all that, of course, was just *English* settlers. Near my own dooryard is the claim-mark of an unknown H. Lougee, carved defiantly deep in the ledge, and dated 1619.

2. Were all Yankees English?

By no means. In colonial times Irish, Welsh and Scotch joined people from England, and to these should be added French, Portuguese, Dutch and Scandinavian and African people. Yankee is *not* a synonym for W.A.S.P.!

3. Was religious freedom the chief reason for coming here?

No. Very, very few came seeking religious freedom. The most impelling reason was hope of a quick fortune. First arrivers — fishermen, for example — had little interest in settlement. The peopling of New England was dictated by a combination of hope for a better life and desperation. Some came neither happily nor willingly, but as victims of the Enclosure Acts, Elizabethan Poor Laws, the English criminal justice system, and famine. Others bound themselves for years of servitude in exchange for a one-way ticket.

4.   Did early Yankees live in log cabins?

No. Or seldom. Frame houses (what is now fashionably called "post and beam") were the rule, the earlier ones walled by clay and wattle (brush) and thatched.

5.   What was a *missioners' glass*?

A magnifying or burning glass. Some missionaries impressed the Indians with the power of the white man's God by kindling fires with them. What they used on cloudy days is not recorded.

6.   What did colonial Yankees do with beaver skins? And tails?

Except when used for coats, the skin itself was discarded, the fur shaved from the hide and made into felt. From this was made the famous "beaver hat." Beaver tails were consumed on the spot by the trapper and considered a great delicacy. The Catholic Church, by the way, officially classified beaver as fish, that trappers might eat the tails with impunity on Fridays.

7.   How big was New England, originally?

From the St. Lawrence to the Chesapeake, and from sea to shining sea, if we put all original patents, grants and claims together. New England colonies claimed against one another as well. Massachusetts grabbed Maine in the 1600s — and hung on till 1820.

8.   What was a *Goshener*?

Gosheners were the first true pioneers, and much of New England (as well as America) owes its settlement to them. These were the Yankees with itchy feet, never long content to stay in any settled place, but seeking some more promising land. To have *gone to Goshen* (a fertile Biblical land) was to have quietly disappeared for parts unknown. They didn't run away, understand; they just got beckoned elsewhere.

9.   Was *wampum* just an Indian form of money?

No. The beaded wampum belt was a badge of office or honor. It was also used for official messages of great importance. Its value came from the great skill and arduous labor in making the beads, usually from seashells, but also from certain stones.

10.   Did most Yankees back the Revolution?

No, not by a long shot. Probably fewer than a third wanted separation from England. Few fought the Revolution clear through, and the Liberty Boys were considered little better than today's terrorists by some.

11. What was a *summer soldier*?

Contrary to even Tom Paine, the summer soldier wasn't the equivalent of a fair-weather friend. Like most other Colonial soldiers, Yankees got their crops into the ground before going off to fight, returning if they could in time for harvest or when their enlistment was up. Many then went back to the tussle, becoming winter soldiers as well. This plan preserved their families and helped keep the troops fed. A torchlight or *pine-knot patriot,* of course, was another matter entirely.

12. Was travelling by *shank's mare* as fast as by *mooseback*?

Yes, they were the same. Shank's mare meant travelling by foot. Moosebacks were moccasins or boots made from the back-hide of the moose, reputedly tougher than the toughest leather and far more pliable.

13. In colonial times, why might you burn your old house down before you moved away?

To recover the nails — in those days nails were made one by one.

14. Could everyone vote at town meeting in early New England?

No. If you owned property above a stated value (£20 or $100 were common averages); if you weren't Jewish, Negro, Catholic or a known agnostic; nor a bound nor indentured servant nor apprentice; had paid your poll tax (not abolished nationally, by the way, till 1964!) and, of course, were not a female, then you probably could vote.

15. Why didn't Vermont sign the Declaration of Independence?

According to one old Vermonter: "Didn't need to. We wuz independent already!" That's undeniable, but the main reason was that Vermont wasn't one of the original thirteen colonies. This Johnny-come-lately held off entering till 1791. They were probably making sure the notion would wash before they got rooked into it. Vermonters never were ones to be dazzled by the new-fangled.

16. Could you travel by turnpike in colonial days?

Yes. Many roads — usually the better, often the only main roads — were privately owned by individuals or companies. A pike or bar was set across the entrance and turned when the fee had been paid. Inns and hostelries along such roads were infamous for their meager comforts and miserly portions, thus our word *piker*. Their prices were *piked up*, too.

17. Was there slavery in colonial New England?

Yes. "Transported" white criminals were almost slaves. Black slavery accounted for up to ten percent of the population of Connecticut, Rhode Island and southern New Hampshire. Slavery was abolished state by state. By 1785 all six were "free states." But citizenship, franchise, education, mobility and the practice of a trade or skill remained sharply restricted in most areas for a century longer.

4.

Dowsers
& Axebenders

Trees, the Kindly Enemy

Acre for acre, New England is still the most heavily forested section of the nation, and Maine the most heavily forested state (ninety percent woods!). To the settler, there seemed to be nothing *but* forest. It was a rare Yankee who could begin farming without having first wrestled this "kindly enemy" at least to a standstill.

See how many of these questions you can wrestle before you're stumped.

1. Were the first Yankees expert woodsmen?

No. They had to become experts, but few began that way. Their first efforts often earned the Indians' amused contempt. The problem was lack of experience. In England, cutting a living tree got you in a lot of trouble. For firewood, the common folks had to make do with what they could get, literally, by hook or by crook. (From this same context, we also get our expression for unexpected good fortune: *windfall*.)

2.   What was a *bowshot* clearing?

The first clearing made around a settler's house or cabin, a bowshot in radius to provide a clear field of fire in case of attack or approach by any stranger. A *bowshot farmer*, a term of contempt, was one who never bothered to clear his land farther. He was likely a *Goshener* at heart anyway, soon to be beckoned elsewhere.

3.   What are *trunnels*?

Literally, tree-nails. Wooden pegs used to hold timbers together in houses, barns or any other timbered structure, including ships. Good for three hundred years.

4.   Name other uses for birch besides canoes.

Birch was one of several "everything" trees, and its uses could fill a book by themselves. As well as canoes, its bark was used for basketry, containers, scoops, measures and boxes; stuffed between outer and inner walls, it made excellent insulation; temporary shelters were often roofed with it. The outer bark of the paper birch was used for exactly that: paper. Birch can be tapped like maples for

syrup and sugar, and the bark and roots are the basic
ingredients for both birch- and root-beer. Black birch is still
tapped for "wintergreen" extract. Birch makes a fair firewood, the handsomest fireplace log, and was formed into all
sorts of *whittles* such as spoons, trenchers, bowls and
leaveners (long trenchers for making bread). Not even
m'aple exceeds its beauty for furniture. Peeled, its brush
makes a fine whisk or eggbeater, and a birch broom was a
staple for hearthsides. It's a favored food tree for partridge
in late winter and for chickadees year-round. Even when
rotten, it's useful (see below, under *punk*). Its finest use is for
swinging on; its worst was by schoolmarms.

5. What was a *stump farm*?

Cutting down trees was one matter; getting the
stumps out was quite another. Land was cultivated between
stumps until they could be pulled. Let them go too long,
though, and you'd be known as a *stump farmer* — first
cousin to the *bowshotter* (above).

6. What tree was the most prized in colonial times?

White oak, though a few make a case for white pine
(and for sassafras, as we'll see later). Oak was essential to
shipbuilding. It was vital not only for ship timbers but,
along with tamarack, for *knees*, the bracings of the ship's
frame hewn from natural bends and crotches of limbs and
brace roots.

7.   Is oak the hardest native wood?

No. Beech, hickory and locust exceed oak for general meanness. But the hardest of all is a little tree, seldom higher than twenty feet or thicker than six inches. Properly called hornbeam, it was also known as *axebender*. It was used for mallets, wedges, some tool handles.

8.   What was a *storm tree*?

Black ash, usually. It has the reputation for attracting lightning. Why, I don't know, but I've lost more ash to thunderbolts than any other species, including next-by and far taller trees. Occasionally, it was planted near dwellings and barns to "draw away" danger.

9.   What firewood burns as well green as dry?

Ash again. In Vermont, making a woman cook with green wood gave her grounds for divorce — but ash was excepted. The much-quoted firewood ditty ends:

> *"...But ash that's green*
> *Or ash that's dry,*
> *A king can warm*
> *his slippers by."*

10. What is *squaw wood*?

Whatever wood that can be picked up without cutting. So called since wood gathering was the female Indian's task (as was most else). Though a term of contempt in New England, squaw wood is not only the quickest to start and the hottest to burn, taking it improves your woodlot.

11. What tree blooms in December?

Witch hazel. It produces spangles of yellow curly blossoms, somewhat like forsythia but smaller and sparser. In size, like hornbeam it's halfway between shrub and tree.

12. What's the best wood for dowsing?

Witch hazel again. It was (still is) the preferred source of dowsers' or diviners' wands, purportedly able to point to water when all others fail. Witch hazel is fraught with all sorts of tales and superstitions, for which it can blame no one but itself: Any tree that blossoms in snowstorms, shoots off its nuts with a bang, and often can't make up its silly mind as to just what shape of leaf it wants is bound to attract attention. Some schoolmarms, by the way, used birch for boys but hazel for girls, girls being more tender-bottomed, perhaps.

13. What wood is slowest to rot?

Locust, especially thorny locust. Mean, hard, stringy, obstinate and nasty to handle in general, it is still tops for jobs half in and half out of water, such as pilings, shoring, bridges, damboxes and so on.

14. What do willow, sassafras, hickory, elm, fir, poplar, hazel and cherry all have in common?

All had (or have) medicinal value of one sort or another. (See *Ox Gall & Onion Candy* below.)

15. Name three uses for *punk*.

Punk is the soft, totally rotted, crumbly innards of stumps and old dead trees, and it was nearly as useful as the tree itself. Yellow birch punk, wrapped in a clamshell and tucked in a mouse skin, would keep a coal of fire alive for three days. It was also the favored tinder for tinderboxes. Apple punk makes the best smoke for curing ham and bacon, even if hickory has hogged all the fame. *Punkwater* — rainwater collected in a punky stump — is, as you must know, a surefire cure for warts; it was also helpful when dealing with those certain signs of Sinful Thoughts, pimples. Dry punk could staunch bleeding, and a brew made from green punk was used as a nerve tonic. Deep jade-green punk glows eerily in the dark, and so sometimes was called *witchwood* or *elfwood*.

16. What was a *king tree*?

A tree blazed with the "broad arrow" of the king and reserved for His Majesty's navy — all trees twenty-four inches in diameter at twelve inches above the ground. This applied not only to the pines prized for masts but to any standing shipwood. Chopping down a king tree was a favorite prank of the Liberty Boys and other early patriots. Dangerous, too: The penalty of 1691 was £100 for every tree.

17. How could you use a tree for a compass?

First, by *not* believing that moss grows thickest on the north side. But trees growing in exposed locations will have their upper branches sheared by the prevailing wind of the region — southwest along most of New England's coasts — and thus will "point" northeast.

18. Where would you find a *whiffletree*?

On a horse. Trees grow but whiffletrees are made. If you *must* know, it is a shortish crossbar swiveled on a clevis at its center and to its nooks or pelvers at either end are fastened the dog links of the traces which lead through luggers in the britchings and the girtle up to the dees of the hames which are chined to the collar by means of which the horse, mare, filly, gelder or nag pulls the buggy, huff, shay, brougham, rig, bucker, ricket, crossacre, waggon, pung, dingle, sleigh, lough, scutter, dray, drag, scoot or harrow. In other words, it's the very thing the Old Gray Mare kicked up many long years ago, when she *was* what she used to be.

5.

Rummage & Wreckers

Maritime Matters

However landbound the Yankee, there is still a trickle of seawater left somewhere in his blood. And while this truth has received perhaps more than its rightful share of attention, here are a few trivia your history books may not have dwelt overlong on.

1. How long was the early passage to New England from Europe?

Six to sixteen weeks, generally. The problem wasn't just the crossing: It was finding out where you were when you got here, as in the case of the *Mayflower*. Columbus, by the way, almost set an all-time record: 36 days. The fast ships of the 1840s could not do much better — but, then, Columbus was on a different, shorter route.

2. What was the navigator's *rule of three L's?*

Early skippers, faced with uncharted waters or wary of the highly imaginative maps of those times, depended on the three L's: *lead, lookout and log.* Lead was cast to measure depth (with the lead often "buttered" with grease to sample the bottom). Lookout was posted not only aloft and in the bows but often sent ahead in the ship's longboat. Log, recording the speed of the vessel, let distances be reckoned from the last-known point.

3. What were *wreckers?*

They were practitioners of a jolly trade probably as old as history: setting up false beacons for inbound ships to steer by, then looting the ships when they wrecked. Not as lucrative as pirating outright, but somewhat safer.

4. Why was beer one of the principal provisions on early sailing vessels?

It was substantially safer than water, which fouled quickly. It was not unusual for a ship to carry as much as 1,500 gallons of beer for a single crossing.

5.   What did it mean to *sail before the mast?*

"Misery" would probably be the best answer. However, sailors before the mast were the "ordinaries" —
common, though able seamen, berthed before (in front of)
the foremast in the fo'c'sle (forecastle).

6.   What might be a principal occupation of a saltwater farmer in winter?

Building a ship. With enough sons, a man could lay
up a fair-sized coaster and, with luck, give up farming
altogether.

7.   What were *letters of marque?*

Letters of marque and reprisal were, in effect, pirate
licenses by which a private vessel (*privateer*) could prey on
the shipping of a country's designated enemy. Both patri-
otic and profitable, albeit a mite risky.

8.   What were *grape, chain* and *cannister?*

Forms of shot for cannon. Grape was a cluster of
small ball shot linked together; chain was two (sometimes
three) larger balls with a length of chain between them
—excellent for messing up spars, masts, and rigging. Cannister was composed of many small balls in a cannister,
tops for spraying enemy decks.

9. Would you boast of an ancestor in *the wool trade*?

Probably not. *The wool trade* was a euphemism for the slave trade, not so much in the *triangle trade* or *three-cornered trade* (see below) as in coastal slaving, which went on into the Civil War. Slaves were often carried on manifests as "bales of wool" to hide the fact not only from ship owners and a myopic government but from Abolitionist wives.

10. You've heard of the Bermuda Triangle, but what was the *triangle trade*?

Again, a reference to slaving, the foundation of many a fine old Yankee family fortune. Many American slavers in the eighteenth and nineteenth century were Yankees and the chief port for the business was New Bedford. Triangle refers to the three passages in the trade. The first was to Africa with rum, which was traded for slaves, who were brought over in the infamous Middle Passage for sale in the West Indies, South America and the southern U.S. In southern parts the ships took on sugar and molasses to be brought back to New England and made into rum — which started the whole cycle over again.

11. If you shipped out as *supercargo*, what were you?

There is much confusion over this term and it's consistently misused. Supercargo meant superintendent of cargo — the ship's business agent. Often a landlubber and a representative of the ship's owners, he was not universally loved, considered a fink or a rat. Masters preferred a *ship's husband* or *husbander*, who performed the same function but usually didn't pesker along on the actual voyage.

12.   What was *rummaging* a ship? Could you hold a sale afterwards?

You could, but few would come to buy. Rummaging meant cleaning out, scrubbing down and fumigating a vessel — an unlovely task, since bilges were used as unofficial toilets. Worst were the slave ships; second worst, fishing vessels, famous for their accumulations of *gurry* or fish slime.

13.   What went into a *slop* chest?

Despite the name, a ship's slop chest held spare clothing for common use and comfort of all hands. Users were expected to contribute something *in kind*, including captains and ship's officers.

Later, in the days of the clippers, the slop chest was run for the captain's private profit, a floating PX, with purchases charged against seamen's wages — comparable to the "company store."

14.   Why would one moor a ship as far up a river as possible?

To kill barnacles, marine borers (teredos or ship-worms) and other hitchhikers, which cannot survive in fresh water. A fouled bottom could cut a ship's speed dramatically.

15. In the old days, would you knit your son or boyfriend mittens to take on a voyage?

Never! Mittens were considered unmanly, womanish, even unlucky, especially on whaling ships.

16. Was there really a whale like *Moby Dick*?

Probably several. The myth of the albino was and still is lodged deeply in almost all folklore. Vermonters had a comparable bad-luck tale of a white deer — a story derived from Indian folklore, probably — which led pursuing hunters to perdition every time. Today in New England, however, a Moby Dick is nothing more than a bulk LP gas storage tank. *Sic transit gloria mundi.*

17. How long could whaling voyages last?

Till all the barrels were filled: Some whaling voyages lasted over four years.

18. What could you get for free in New England winters that had demand the world around?

Ice. Artificial ice was unknown until well into the 1850s and rare as a regularly delivered product. Yankees cut ice for their own use, but even more for export. It was still being cut on the Kennebec River in Maine in the 1930s. Shipped as far away as Calcutta, it was almost worth its weight in Poland Water, which also had a wide market and was from Maine.

19. Who was the meanest New England captain of all time?

There'll be argument over this, but many said it was
Floyd Ireson of Marblehead, a whaling captain who ignored
another Marblehead ship's distress in order to beat home for
the best market. The ladies of Marblehead corrected his
error, as told in the old chant:

> Old Floyd Ireson, for his hard heart,
> Tarred and feathered and carried in a cart
> By the women of Marblehead...

Or, if you'd have it in the original dialect, here it is as I
learned it when a wee child in that noble town:

> Ald Flerd Errisun far 'is 'arrd 'eart,
> Turred and fithert un carrd in a currt
> Bay the weemen o' Mobble'ood...

Whether they also *rocked him 'round the corner* —
Marblehead's version of the Welcome Wagon — I don't
know. Rocking 'round the corner was when kids ambushed
strangers with rocks.

20. How did a *wet widow* differ from a dry one?

A dry widow was one whose husband was safe and
sound in the family graveyard, where she could keep her eye
on him. But more than one woman whose husband failed to
return with his ship, from having gotten himself drowned
on the voyage, harbored the suspicion that he might have
jumped ship to start a new and wifeless life elsewhere.

While she kept an eye wet for him, one widowed
ancestor of mine held through forty years and two more
husbands that her Willimus was all too alive and doing all
too well somewhere, and she'd live to give him his come-

uppance yet. Rumor has it she caught up with him in San Francisco, where he'd gone in the Gold Rush, and dragged him home to die proper.

21. Were *widow walks* built so wives could watch for the return of their husbands' ships?

No, they were built for chimneysweeps and in the event of fire. These rooftop walkways were built on houses far inland, and their purpose was to give ready access to the chimneys. Sweeps charged a penny less for the convenience.

22. Would you whistle a tune when a ship's underway?

Never, unless the ship was dead-becalmed. Then you might try to whistle up a wind. Otherwise, whistling encouraged gales and contrary winds, but songs or chanties were fine anytime.

6.

Pelfers
& Potmeat

The Yankee as Hunter

Anyone who ventures into the outlands of New England in the fall finds a peculiar quiet there, a waitingness in everything. Voices drop, ears perk, eyes turn sharp. The ridges are being walked again. I am not speaking of the current visible hunter, often fresh up from the City in a splash of Day-Glo, all Beaned out from head to toe and toting firepower enough for a middle-sized war. I'm speaking of that ineffable and ancient shade, the Yankee hunter.

Perhaps these questions will help you to know him just a little better, before he's mistaken for a "sportsman."

1.   What was a *pelfer*?

Another name for a trapper, a man who hunted for pelts (pelfry). The first to open up the wilderness to the settler, he was a different breed of Yankee — when he stayed in one place long enough to become a Yankee. The fur trade promised quick riches — for everyone but those who risked their necks getting the furs to begin with.

2.   Why did pelfers and other Yankees not get along?

The trapper too often *went Injun*, and what friends he acquired wouldn't quite fit in at, say, a church "sociable." Many married Indian girls and so were *set apart*, written out of the family history. Neither side seemed to mind too much, actually.

3.   In the old days, what pelt was the most valuable?

Traditionally, beaver — until the silk hat took over the fashion in the early 1800s. Mink was not fashionable in any great degree, and the varmints weren't worth the bother. Ermine — which is only the weasel in his white winter coat and black tail — were for royalty, but fetched no special price to the trapper at least. Coonskins at one point were six to the dollar; red fox barely better. But a silver fox was a prize, sometimes worth as much as twenty beaver for a single pelt.

4.   What was the most useful pelt?

Buckskin, with rabbit a steady second. A set of buckskins could last a man a dozen years, helped along by grease on the outside and sweat within. (For more about buckskin and rabbit, see *Pokes & Buskins*.)

5.   What was a *deadfall*?

A heavy log teetered up so as to fall when the bait below was triggered. Set mainly for bear. Pitfalls, deep lightly-covered holes baited in the middle, were used seldom. But snares were common: No one wasted good gunpowder on a rabbit.

6.   What was a pelfer's *tormentation*?

No one ever knew why it took place and the man himself would never say. A tormentation was a vendetta between the man and a particular kind of animal and sometimes a particular animal. Though not on so grand a scale, it was like what Ahab felt toward Moby Dick. A tormented pelfer forsook all other pursuits to seek the animal out, regardless of season or loss. Foxes were common tormentors, with bear and lynx, bobcat and wolf sharing honors. But not all objects of pursuit were dangerous. Raccoon and porcupine came in for their share of hate, and one New Hampshire fellow spent a dozen years trying to track down a buck who'd chased him up a tree. (He didn't succeed.)

7.   Would old-time hunters ever whisper?

Never. Speak low instead. As any good hunter will tell you, "A whisper will lie in the grass and hiss till sundown."

8.   What was *trotting* a deer?

Serious hunters trotted deer — paralleled the deer's daily circuits from cover to feed to water, gradually moving in closer. Done regularly, the herd would take the hunter's presence for granted. When needed, he just went and collected. The term is still used, largely in disdain of "sportsmen" who flounder all over the woods and come out empty handed, but the fine art of trotting is now little known and less practiced.

9.   What was *pemmican*?

Any iron ration, but chiefly dried meat, suet or fat, berries and sometimes nuts, all chopped together and packed hard into a skin or gut. An Indian invention lasting almost indefinitely, it could be boiled or gnawed at as you went. Mincemeat is a vague relation, but no one ever baked a pemmican pie!

10.   How were wild ducks preserved for winter eating?

They were skinned, then all but the breasts were thrown away, and these were packed raw in kegs, with boiling lard poured over them. Would keep a year. Just dig out a duck whenever you want one and pour in more lard to fill the hole.

11. How was meat smoked if you didn't have a smokehouse?

Inverted *hogsheads* (very large barrels) were used for small batches. But often chimneys had a smoke chamber built into them for the purpose. One old lady in Maine only allowed her husband to smoke a pipe if he sat under the chamber with the door open.

12. What was *potmeat*?

Whatever would fit in the pot. See next question.

13. What was *Brunswick stew*?

I've heard this argued, and I've heard it all fancied up. But I still hold that it's rabbit, partridge and squirrel all *seethed* together, and if one is missing, it isn't Brunswick stew. And don't clutter it up with a lot of herbs, either.

14. What animal eats porcupines?

Fishers are the only animals that have perfected methods of killing and eating porcupines without getting a mouthful of quills. They aim for the "soft underbelly" where no quills grow, then eat the poor chap by rolling his skin inside out as they go.

15. What use are porcupines to humans?

Nothing in nature is useless. Porkies are messy eaters and, in deep snow, the twigs and branches they drop provide fodder for rabbits and deer, which feed humans. They are also about the only animal that a desperate and weaponless man can kill easily for survival rations in the wild. Porcupine livers are large, tender, delicious and are best eaten raw. Or so I hear.

16. What's *muffle*?

Moose lips. Most delicate part of the whole beast.

17. How did Indians pack out a thousand-pound moose?

They didn't. They just moved their family to the moose. A *moosecamp* was a term, somewhat derisive, for any temporary or tumble-down dwelling, or portion thereof: "Her kitchen's a regular moosecamp!"

18. What's the difference between a *decoy* and a *toller*?

Life itself. A toller was a live duck with its wing-feathers clipped to prevent its flying off. Every duckhunter of decent persuasion kept a dozen or so. It was considered poor sport to bag your own toller. They are now forbidden, like most everything else useful.

19. Loons are entirely inedible and impossible to bag anyway. Why, then, would a duckhunter use a loon decoy?

The loon is the most cautious of all waterbirds. Ducks, spying the "loon" just floating there at his ease, presumed the coast was clear. That's probably forbidden, too, now. Should be. It's a nasty trick.

7.
Pitfrawls & Twivels

The Crafty Yankee

The Yankee reputation for craftsmanship is well-deserved, but craftsmanship seemed perfectly ordinary in the old days, and highly necessary: Little could be bought ready-made, nor was there money to buy it. Planned obsolescence had not yet been invented, so the rule was *do it once the one right way*. Detroit would do well to adopt that for a motto.

1.   What was a *joiner*?

Pronounce it as you may — joiner, *jointer, jiner, jintiner* — he was a skilled carpenter, since "all" there is to carpentry, when you come to think of it, is joining together pieces of wood.

2. Why might a joiner mark his toolbox with a cross?

To remind himself that he was working at the Lord's trade. It seemed to work: Carpenters were known for softer voices, honest dealing and fewer cusswords than fellow craftsmen.

3. Could you build a cabin with only an axe?

Yes. One good axe, with a good man at the end of the handle, could do "everything but bore holes and milk the cow..." They weren't, but they *could* be used to shave with. The axe was the first tool. If you learned its uses properly, all other tools were just to help it out.

4. What did it mean to *hew to the line*?

To stay true to the line marked on a log when squaring it into a timber. No easy matter, since a log tapers but a beam mustn't. Some could hew true without a line. If you *hewed to your own line*, it meant either that you minded your own business, made up your own rules, or went at things your own way.

5. How true could a man hew?

To within a quarter inch, often less — not much coarser than a modern sawmill.

6.   What was a *mortise and tenon*?

The main method of joining timbers (and much else, all the way down to fine furniture). The mortise is the square hole, the tenon the part that fits into it. Also known as joining things *Tom and Sally*, the mortise being female, the tenon male. Such joints were usually secured with *trunnels*, which we mentioned earlier.

7.   How did a trunnel work?

It didn't just hold mortise and tenon together; it also drew them together. The trunnel holes in the tenon never quite lined up with those through the mortise, so when the trunnel was driven home, it forced the timbers even more tightly together. You can't pull a trunnel out of the beams easily until the beams rot away.

8.   In olden days, would you leave the beams in your house exposed?

Good Lord, never! The modern rage to expose the beams in old houses is like going to town with your britches down. When not lathed and plastered proper, beams were always *dressed* with well-planed boards, carefully chamfered (planed at an angle to fit together at the edges) and painted or whitewashed. Naked beams were allowable only in barns, sheds, cellars and summer kitchens.

9.   Why did old-time Yankees shy away from iron plows?

In the belief — held outside New England, too — that iron "poisoned" the soil. Only the share (the point of the plow) might be metal or metal faced.

10. Yankee tools are notable for their names. Here's a chance to pick up some extra stumps if you can tell what these were: *slick; twivel; scorp; snath; frow; butteris; commander*. That's seven extra stumps if you get them all; otherwise, one stump for each right answer, though it's a good chance to earn a fool or two.

A *slick* is a long, heavy chisel, used for cutting mortises, which would be *fined up* sometimes with a *twivel*, a one-handed tool with a head like a slightly curved chisel and a handle set at right angles to it (on the order of a hatchet). Smaller mortises could be cut with the twivel alone. A *scorp* is another matter entirely, a short-handled, curved-edge tool somewhat like a small adze, used to scorp (scoop) out the innards of things like bowls, log troughs and trenchers. Coopers (barrel makers) used a more refined version for smoothing out the staves of the barrel once assembled. Gutters for eaves were scorped from a length of cedar. A *snath* is the long, curved handle for a scythe. Also called a *sneeth* or *snid*. The *nibs* were the handles you held it by. A *frow* (or froe) was used for splitting off shingles from a *balk*, a short log (preferably of cedar). It was a long blade with one end turned up and formed into a handle, and a squared back of the blade that was *mauled* (struck with a mallet) to drive the frow through. Shakes as well as shingles could be made with a frow, but as often they were struck off with a *broadaxe* (the axe used for hewing). A *butteris* is a tool used for paring the hooves of horses. A *commander* is a very large mallet, often fashioned from a tree limb with a section of trunk, the limb serving as its handle.

11. And while we're at it, just what, pray tell, is a *pitfrawl*?

Any tool or part that no one knows the use of or reason for anymore. Such are sometimes also called shalbibs, thuls, swicks, fretcleaves or naveknappers. There's a nasty rumor that old-time blacksmiths used to make such things in their spare time and toss them out in the countryside just to mystify future generations.

12. What was a *dog*?

Just about anything, it seems. *Raft dogs* were used to hold logs together when they were rafted. These were iron bars, with each end bent and sharpened. Dogs also were used in sawmills to hold the log being sawn; cruder cousins of these secured a log for hewing. Smaller ones were on every workbench. Not all dogs had teeth, however. I've heard a peg or trunnel called a dog, and a *dogpost* or just a dog was the last prop knocked out when a boat was launched, so to be *at the dog-end* of a job meant the more risky or less pleasant part of it, which may explain why an under-bright apprentice was called the *dogboy*.

13. Did blacksmiths mainly shoe horses?

No. They would do it only grudgingly or maybe not at all. To a true smith, horses (and oxen) were the province of the *farrier*. Smiths made things, repaired things and best of

all invented things. They were the original Yankee tinker-
ers, not the *tinker*, who repaired only pots and pans.

14. What was the farrier's main other skill?

The farrier was the veterinarian or a reasonable
facsimile thereof, and doubtless made more of a reputation,
if not money, by his linaments, tonics and remedies than by
his shoeings. When you took a horse to be shod, it was
expected that he'd also get a free check-up. (See the chapter
Ox Gall & Onion Candy.)

15. Was whittling just a pastime?

Not at all: a true Yankee did nothing but useful
things, remember. Kitchen items and other small useful
things that *weren't worth the waste of daylight* were made
in those long winter evenings, as much by feel as by sight.
In more liberated households, toys, *gimcracks, hoodles* and
other *codgerings* might be tolerated on grounds of making
shavings for kindling the fire.

16. Why would a Yankee hoard up iron filings?

Soaked in vinegar till they dissolved, they made up
into a fine black ink. This is the now-faded, pale-brown,
rusty-colored ink you see on old documents and letters.

17. ...and bits of broken glass?

Finest thing for scraping surfaces smooth, particularly tool handles. When the edge dulls, just crack off a piece for a new edge. A good axehandle, for example, was *culleted* till it was smooth as the glass that smoothed it.

18. Why were Yankees less concerned about muddy, rutted roads than folks nowadays?

They weren't in such a hellfire hurry to get places might be one answer. But the real reason was the wheels they used. Seldom less than four feet in diameter, it had a purchase or leverage of two feet or better (a wheel, in terms of physics, is a "continuous lever"). Your car is lucky to have seven inches. Besides, if a cart got stuck, you could always *walk the spokes* to help Old Dobbin out.

19. Why would you always keep a hammer in a sled or sleigh?

For a snowknocker, naturally! Horses' hooves (if shod) *ball up*, snow accumulating in a hard-packed ball so high the *caulkins* of the shoe can't get a grip. Just stop, heist a hoof and knock out the ball, or scorp it out with the nether end of the snowknocker. Special hammers were made just for this, designed to hang on harness or saddle.

8.

Jillies & Quintals

Weights and Measures

Not only the finest kind of noun, *Yankee* is the best of all possible adjectives as well. Anything *Yankee made* will last till Doomsday; a job done *Yankee fashion* is done the one right way. And to be given *Yankee measure* is to get *full, fair and a palm more.*

So while bureaucrats and schoolmarms may metrify the rest of America, the Yankee (let us hope) will disabuse such bosh. What liter could ever better a *pottle*? What dull kilometer match a *country mile*?

1. Just how far is a *country mile*?

The only thing certain is that it will never be less than the 5,280-foot statute mile. And generally more. A country mile is reckoned in time as well as distance ("Oh, a person could be a good hour at it...") since a mile in summer is in no way the equal of a mile in winter or mud season. Pesker too hard about exactitudes and you may be told that a country mile is exactly twice as long as halfway-there, but only half as far as there-and-back. Most country miles, however, run from where-you-be till when-you-get-there.

2. Could you carry your bride over the threshhold if she was twenty *stone* with a twelve-*span* waist?

No. Only with the help of every bridesmaid you can muster. A stone is fourteen pounds and a span the distance from end of thumb to the tip of little finger — eight to ten inches or so. So your bride would weigh two hundred and eighty pounds and be, at kindest, ninety-six inches round her middle.

3. How far from shore is a ship when she's *hull under*?

Hull under is that distance from shore (or from another ship) when a ship's hull appears to drop under the curve of the earth (also called *hull down*). Exact distance depends on where you're standing, of course, but man-high at sea level would be about seven miles. However, when a person's hull under, it means he's imbibed a mite more than he should have. If someone's *gone hull under*, it's a general decline, like old age, and maybe he's "just about *slipped his moorings*." But hull under can also mean the same as "out of sight, out of mind," as in: "He warn't hull under before she'd put her beck to that Bailey boy..."

4.   Would you keep fish in a *firkin*?

You don't let a fish even into the same pantry as a firkin! A *firkin* is a small wooden tub for butter (sometimes lard), and to *keep a fish in a firkin* is the ultimate in slutty housekeeping. To be above one's ordained social heights was to be *as out of place as a fish in a firkin*. All this, of course, because the mildest of fish would impart a flavor to the tub no butter could withstand. Domestic firkins came in all sizes, but the commercial breed held a fourth *(firth)* of a barrel, about fifty pounds.

5.   Your home is a *riding* away. Could you make it there before dark?

Yes, if you started early enough. Like a country mile, a riding was no exact measure, just roughly the distance of a day's ride on horseback, and that of course depended on horse, road and rider.

If the rider was a preacher, however, riding meant the circuit he rode, and that could be a hundred miles or more. *Riding seven Sundays* meant that the Sabbath was whatever day the preacher arrived in a settlement having no regular church and parson. One old circuit preacher in Vermont held services back to back — two "Sundays" in a row: worship and funerals the first day, weddings and dippings (baptismals) the second. One old New Hampshire lady told her dying husband: "Lorimer, ye'd better do it soon. Preacher's due round tomorry an' kin put ye under proper..." Made old Lorimer mad enough to live another thirty years.

6.   How many in a *Yankee dozen*?

Same as in a baker's dozen: thirteen. The extra item

was for sampling, so you could still go home with a full dozen and be sure of what you'd bought. "Even" dozens were given only by pikers such as today's commercial bakeries.

7.   What was a *walking purchase*?

Just another way to cheat the Indians. A walking purchase was the amount of land that might be walked around in a single day. Indians had little comprehension of real estate. Property, to them, was literally what could be carried, and who could carry mountain, meadow, forest or river? One such purchase in Vermont was ten miles to the side — a hundred square miles in all — and it was the work of a professional walker brought in expressly for the job. Rumor had it that the "walker" was actually a set of twins, one of whom set out the day before, rested up at the halfway point, relieved his brother and blazed his way back to the start as the "same" man.

8.   If you were sitting *fifty hands high*, what would be under you?

A horse, and a mighty high horse at that. Hand was (and still is) the unit of measure of a horse's height from ground to withers. Hand came from the width, not the length, of a hand, now standardized at four inches. So a fifty-hand horse would be made mostly of your own fine opinion of yourself, and for such *high-handed* antics your neighbors would likely help you down from your *high horse*.

9.   What is a *quarter section*?

A *quarter section* is one hundred and sixty acres, or

one-fourth of a *section*, which is a square mile and which, in turn, is one-thirty-second of a *township*. The measure is still used. It was considered the optimum amount of land needed for the subsistence of a family. What kind of land was not reckoned into the measure, however. One executor's inventory listed the deceased's holdings as "two quarter-sections, six acres tillable..." But that, of course, could only happen in New Hampshire.

10. Would you do business with a man who *meted* to the last *link*?

Yes. He'd be a very honest fellow indeed; he just wouldn't be more than honest. To mete, as any Bible-reader knows, is to measure out. A link is 7.92 inches, the length of a link in a surveyor's chain which, for some reason, is sixty-six feet long, thus containing a hundred links. To mete to the last link was to give full but precise measure. *To have a few extra links* in your chain was to take a mite more than was due, and to measure with a *slack chain* was to cheat outright.

11. Could you navigate in ten *marks* of water?

Yes, even with a battleship. Mark is another word for *fathom* — six feet — in some speech, but correctly it refers to the *bunts* of cloth or leather tied onto a sounding line by which water depth was measured. The tenth mark would generally denote twenty-five fathoms or a hundred and fifty feet of water. Probably could risk it even at low tide.

12. What came in a *quintal*?

Fish — split, salted and dried. Whether you care to pronounce this one *kwintal* or *kintle* or *kantle* or *kunnel*, it will still weigh a hundred pounds. It well may be the oldest surviving measure for fishermen. It comes from the Arabic *qintar* and was borrowed from them by the Portuguese and Spanish who might have been fishing the New England coasts many years before Columbus.

13. How many *gills* to a *pottle*?

In this case, gills aren't those things fish wear under their chins, and the word's pronounced *jill*. Slightly more than enough to float a tadpole, it is technically one-fourth of a pint — thus an eighth of a quart and a sixteenth of a pottle, two of which made a gallon. The womenfolk always favored the pottle (half-gallon) jug for kitchen use, especially for maple syrup and molasses; menfolks had other notions about what should go in 'em. Thus a fellow who'd imbibed an untameable amount might be said to be *pottled*. A gill or *jillie*, on the other hand, came to mean anything smallish and full of sweetness, particularly a girl. Thus a lad might get himself *all decked out jillie-go* — dressed up in his best to go see some jillie.

9.

Pippins
& Limbertwigs

The New England Apple

Folks who know only "store-bought" apples have yet to scratch the peel of true Appledom. As with Yankees themselves, no two Yankee apples were alike. Even scions from the same mother tree, planted a few farms apart, grew separate adjectives and fiercely partisan adherents. You could eat your apple-a-day for a year and never taste the same flavor twice. It's not the clam or the lobster but the apple that holds the true flavor of New England.

1. Name five kinds of apples besides MacIntosh, Delicious, Winesap and Cortland.

Well, just for starters, there are Baldwin, Russet, Pearmane, Northern Spy, Astrakhan, Wolfe River, Davey, Sweet Greening, Romes, Melton, Granny Smith, Snow, Jeniton, Chanego, Smokers, Chimney, Morton, Costard, Magnum Bonum (a.k.a. both Bonnies and Maggies), Jonathan Fameuse ("Moose" to Yankees), Gillflower, Wealthy, Transparent, Albermarle, Limbertwig, fourteen kinds of Crab, and that ultimate apple of a dozen definitions, the Seek-No-Further. Then, of course, there were *crosses* of each, and *double-crosses* and *sports* and *escapes*.

2. What was an escape?

An apple that had "escaped" from the orchard and gone off into the woods to live by itself. No proper Yankee ever cut down a wild apple until he had first tasted its fruit. Even then, most escapes were left as *tollers*: They tolled (enticed) deer to them in the fall during hunting season.

3. Can you name five apple dishes?

Besides just apple pie and applesauce, there's apple huff (a one-crust apple pie), apple spiders, apple cobbler, apple duff, apple crisp, apple porcupine, apple boater, apple tricks or *trikes*, apple basters, apple fritters, apple tarts, apple nippers, apple betty, apple turnabouts; puffs, potties, syrup, jam, jelly and butter, fritters, panners, flap-jacks, *doughnaughts*, larrups and do-si-dos.

4.   What is the best use of peels and cores?

These were the soul of good jelly, adding not only color but flavor from the seeds. The Astrakan, red-streaked clear through, was the prize jelly apple. Peels and cores were also cooked and *dripped* (strained through a jellybag; sometimes worked through a sieve) for apple syrup which, boiled down further, became apple taffy. Apple butter always included peels and cores, not in the final product but in the mast from which it was made.

5.   What was a pippin?

Some held it was a breed of apple in itself, with some appropriate adjective like sweet pippin, winter pippin, horse pippin. Some held that a pippin was an apple with flavor enough for jelly and pectin enough for jellying. But mostly, pippin was (and still should be) a superlative, an apple that's a real *pip*. Small boys had their own definition; see below.

6.   How did old-time Yankees preserve apples?

Aside from jelly, jam and apple butter, apples were also *napped* — peeled, cored, sliced and strung up to dry somewhat on the order of apple schnitz; these were sometimes called *pronged* apples. Then there was apple *potty*, raw apple slices preserved in sugar with a dash of cinnamon and a scatter of whole cloves. But many apples were *keepers* which, properly sorted and stored, kept through till spring, getting winier by the hour and permeating the whole house. *Mayapple* didn't refer to the wildflower of that name, but to any apple that would keep through till the following May, when rhubarb could take over in the pie department.

7. In the old days, why would you polish apples (besides for teachers)?

Polished on wool — raw wool if possible — apples would keep considerably longer. Surface molds were wiped off and perhaps a thin layer of lanolin added. This treatment was only for *eaters* or *hand-apples*, often hung up by their stems in the cellar.

8. What were *buckers* or *buck-apples*?

Apples used as stuffers for game — chopped whole, they would "draw" the gaminess from wild duck, turkey, partridge and, especially, *buckmeat*, venison from a ronky old buck deer. They were discarded before cooking, of course.

9. What good are crab apples?

Aside from making their own jelly, they were added to almost any other kind of jelly to provide pectin, without which jelly won't *set*.

10. Why might you keep an apple or two in your closet?

To repell clothes moths. To do that, you made a *clove-apple*, an apple pierced with whole cloves till the whole surface was covered. A clove apple would last a good half-dozen years.

11. What was the main reason the old Yankees grew so many apple trees?

For cider. Cookery, eatery, even jellery were only fringe benefits. Water was considered unhealthful, and cider replaced it for drinking.

12. Why did Yankees relish cider so much?

Frankly, because, unlike water, left to itself for a little while, cider took on an "edge." Freshly pressed cider is nothing but apple juice. But given the chance it would ease its way into true ciderhood. Cider, if the truth be told, is essentially apple wine.

13. Just what is *hard cider*?

Cider gone so *edgy* it's stopped *working*, stopped fizzing with fermentation. *Bunger* was truly hard cider, a bit dreggy but with surprising impact. *Hop cider* was not made by adding hops, as with beer, but cider just naturally as bitter as it was sour. Powerful.

14. What was *applejack*?

The Yankee's answer to the Southerner's *white lightning* or *panther sweat*, and a far cry from the "applejack" peddled in likker stores today. Hard cider run through a still is merely apple brandy. True applejack is — or at least used to be — made by freezing a barrel of fully hard cider. The barrel was then bored with an auger and what cider remained liquid in the center was *augered off*. Since alcohol won't freeze even in a Yankee winter, what you eventually got was close to pure spirits. Good applejack was the product of at least three augerings, each augering frozen in turn till there just wasn't anything left to freeze. It was jugged and kept stashed in the barn away from the Old Woman's pryings.

15. Why would someone keep her hundred-year-old mother tightly bunged up in a barrel in her cellar?

So the mother wouldn't *wane*. Mother (in this case) means mother-of-vinegar, a clotty grayish mass of algae which turns cider into vinegar. Some Yankee families kept a *strain* going for over a century, and were famous for it. A *clot* of mother added to a barrel of cider would *work* it in only a few weeks, but vinegar was not truly aged and fit for human use till it was *eeled* — with vinegar eels: tiny, hairlike nematodes.

16. How do you whip apples?

Never with blender or eggbeater! First, you need an applesnapper, a long willowy whip, smoothly sharpened at its small end. Next you need pippins, in this case meaning the little immature apples that drop off in early summer. The pippin is stuck on the snapper's point and sent sailing with a smart snap of the whip. Range: up to three hundred yards; one can be very accurate with practice and the right kind of pippins. A good applesnapper and two pocketsworth of pippins can get a boy into almost any kind of trouble. Go try it.

10.

Jonahs & Doormats

Fish — the Mainstay

Fish form only a small part of the Yankee diet today, and much of it comes canned or frozen. Perhaps like anything too plentiful and too familiar, fish bred the Yankee's contempt. More likely, they were a reminder of poor times, when seafood wasn't a choice but a necessity. As one old Mainer put it: "There's fish, and then there's *real* vittles..." In token of that sentiment, I'm giving each its own batch of trivia, serving the fish course first.

1.   What is *stockfish*?

Stockfish is the original name for salt or sun-dried fish — cod, hake, haddock, pollock and the like — split and cured on *flakes* (racks) and so sometimes called *flakefish*. Now it is sold in little wooden boxes, or readied up in cans and called codfish cakes by strangers, just *cod cakes* by Yankees.

2. If you were an apprentice in the old days, would you eat salmon often?

Four times a week perhaps. Old indentures (contracts between apprentice and master) sometimes stipulated that the poor lad would not be forced to eat the things more often. Almost too plentiful, they were never a great favorite, being of such a "wrong" color. But *Kennebec salmon* (as often taken in the Penobscot) were world-renowned and a major export before pollution set in.

3. Why do peas and salmon go together on the Fourth of July?

This traditional New England dish has no close relationship to Independence Day itself. Any farmer worth his salt always had green peas by the Fourth (and still does); the first real runs of salmon took place at the same time.

4. How could you tell when mackerel were back and biting?

When lightning bugs began their summer's blinkings. A *tinker* — the smallest and best mackerel — wouldn't think of coming in sight of land until he saw them. And still won't.

5.   If you are offered a batch of fresh codfish heads, should you feel insulted?

Not in the least. Cheeks and tongues — also called *jowls* and *collops* — were once and still should be considered a great delicacy. Nor would you think of wasting the rest of the head. Heads, minus gills, and any other part of the fish save scales and guts, were bagged up tight, tossed into a kettle of boiling water and *seethed* (simmered) for a day on the back of the stove. Add peppercorns, bay leaf and salt, go empty the bag for the cats, and by the time you're back you've got *jonah*, fishdom's answer to the bouillion cube.

6.   Is an *alewife* a spouse too fond of drink?

This should be a question anybody can answer. Alewives are a breed of large herring, usually caught in their spring runs back up to fresh-water spawning grounds. Caught by the bushel, smoked and sold by the string, there is nothing finer to gnaw on when washed down with ale or beer.

7.   Just how might you cook a *doormat*?

Any way you'd cook a flounder, for a doormat is just a flounder as big as a doormat — maybe one trying to work his way up to halibut. One of the finest ways to cook one (or any such fish) is to gut the fish, cake it in clay, set it on top of coals, heap more coals over it, and let it bake till the clay's hard. Then crack it open. Skin and scales stick to the clay; the rest is just pure eating.

8.   Did Yankees actually eat eels?

Fried, baked, pickled, jugged, kegged, kenched, jellied, smoked and aspicked, eels were once a common delight on many a Yankee table. Today, there are still a few *eelers* but, sadly, their catches are almost entirely exported. Just what caused eel's decline in favor is not known. Word may have gotten out about how they used to be caught: The body of a dead animal was deeply gashed, then thrown overboard with a rope tied to it. Hoisted up now and then, the eels would be plucked from the gashes and the bait tossed back for refills. *Eelskins*, by the way, were used for door hinges. I've seen them outlast the door itself.

9.   Do decent people eat *mudroaches* today?

Indeed they do — and at premium prices. But decent people didn't use to. *Mudroach* is an original Yankee name for lobster, a creature so despised it was thought proper food only for hens and paupers — in that order. They were not caught in pots but taken by hand at low tide, usually by children, and sneaked in the back door. Their consumption was thought a sure sign of poor skill at real fishing.

10.   Are mussels a native Yankee food?

Ye gods, no! Although the most plentiful and surely the most easily gathered, they were once thought to be poison, though "furriners" might eat them with impunity. Now fast becoming a major industry in places, the True Yankee still disdains them.

11. Did Yankees used to eat tuna?

Never. In the Old Days — that is, up to about thirty years ago — tuna were known as *horse mackerel* and were shot for the damage they might cause seines. Wholly inedible anyway, as were mako, bluefish and even cusk. It's amazing how their flavor has improved lately!

12. What made the great Yankee herring industry decline?

Don't blame the high cost of labor or foreign competition entirely. Blame it more on changing tastes. Did *you*, for instance, have your poached kipper or sprats for breakfast this morning? One reason was the advent of "real" meat from the West; another was the end of slavery by the Civil War. Herring, pickled (*kenched*), or just salted down, were a main food for slaves both in the South and the West Indies (where stockfish also was the rule). Planters (including George Washington) worked out the cheapest and most efficient "balanced" feed for slaves: corn, fatpork and herring.

11.

Squibs & Duff

The Yankee Menu

Never plain but nothing fancy was the rule for old-time Yankee Cookery. With limited ingredients and unlimited demands on her, the Yankee housewife laid a table which stands as a quiet triumph. It is still not properly celebrated, perhaps because, with the exception of a few basic dishes, it never constituted a formal "cuisine." While favorites, usually bordering on the fancy, were passed along, written down, and have been collected, the everyday *vittlins* were taken for granted and so soon forgotten. Even the names sound queer — *duff, solimer, tardy* — to a present world where most have never tasted kidneys or tripe or *sowbelly* and where puddings are only for dessert. What follows may give you some notions for experimenting on your own.

1.   Just what was *duff*, anyway?

Duff is another word for dough, though more often it was a batter into which almost anything might be tossed, stirred and then cooked. If cooked as it was in a pot, it was just duff. Poured into a bag and boiled, it was *pudding*, the bag being peeled off and the contents served by the slice. If it was leavened a mite, rolled out, filled, rolled up again and baked, it was *solimer* — though where that word comes from, I don't know. The *plum duff* spoken of by sailors was only wistful irony: The duff they got was hardly made with plums. But duff can be as fancy as you want: take blueberry duff for an example. I'd say duff's universal quality is that it is solid and chewy, like real dumplings should be — which I've heard called *dufflings*, by the way.

2.   What does it mean: *no cow, no kitchen*?

Although few grown-up Yankees were much for drinking milk, the cow was the keystone of the home economy. From her came milk, cream, butter, cheese and their cousins buttermilk, cottage cheese, *bonny clabber* (curds and whey) and *clotty* (the almost-solid cream from the top of a well-chilled crock). From the *skimmin's* came the slops for hogs and chickens and, mixed with ochre, paint.

3.   What did the old Yankees use for sweetening?

There isn't much evidence that Yankees used less sweetening than we use today, they just used different kinds. Refined sugar was sold by the loaf, *spanjered* (or grated) off as needed, or broken off in lumps. Bees were kept — our large bumblebee is an import from England, where its proper name was humble, not bumble — and wild honey was not a rarity: Most regions had a *honeyman* expert at lining out wild bees' nests, which could yield as much as a hundred pounds of honey. Maple sugar and syrup were made, of course, and birch in areas too northerly or too high to grow maples. The finest sweetener was *weepings:* A hollow would be made in the top of a firkin of maple sugar and clear, deep, heavy syrup would "weep" out and fill the hollow. But the mainstay sweetener was molasses (or *treacle*). And if you ran out of all these, you could boil down a batch of *sugar pumpkins*, not oversweet but very good.

4.   What really was *hasty pudding*?

Cornmeal mush, boiled till thick, cooled, sliced, fried and, properly, doused with molasses. Go try it.

5.   Did the old Yankees eat a lot of potatoes?

Not at first. It took nearly two centuries for potatoes to become a staple food. Grains and corn were considered far more dependable and were stored and transported more readily. Potatoes were snubbed as "lower class" food, thought (sometimes rightly) to be untrustworthy.

6.   Did the early Yankees eat tomatoes?

The tomato or *pomme d'amour* (love apple) was grown strictly as an ornamental and considered deadly poison for years. Now New England grows a truly fine tomato, so fine we eat 'em all and export not a one.

7. Did eighteenth- and nineteenth-century Yankees can a lot of their food?

No, not till late in the last century. The Yankee "ate with the season." Some ignoramuses have remarked on the "dourness" of the Yankee garden. Not so. Land was limited and labor as much so, so the effort went into *keepers* — pumpkin, squash, cabbage, turnips, onions, carrots and the like. Any "summer" vegetable was favored as long as it would also make up into a "winterable" crop. Thus, peas, beans, beets, turnips and corn lived a double life, good green in summer but also usable in the cold season. What an old-time Yankee would do with zucchini I'd rather not say.

8. What was the Yankee's first spring vegetable?

Parsnips. Not worth eating unless they've been left in the ground all winter. Then, dug up as soon as frost would allow, they were baked with butter and a healthy sprinkle of sugar. The second spring vegetable was dandelion greens (boiled in three waters, dowsed with vinegar and drizzled with salt pork); fast on its heels came rhubarb which, as mentioned, signalled the end of the Apple Season.

9. Did Yankees eat many wild foods?

Yes. A true Yankee eats what's edible — edible to a Yankee. Besides dandelion and fiddleheads, he (more likely she) garnered many wild greens for *salet* (what we call salad) including watercress, shepherd's purse, purselain, sorrel. But the king of all greens was the milkweed, taken in three stages of growth. First, the shoots; second, the unopened flowerballs; third, the baby pods — nature's wild answer to, respectively, asparagus, broccoli and okra. Daylily buds were also taken (delicious raw or fried in batter) which may help account for the large patches of them still found around old farmyards.

10. What was a *hoecake*?

Reputedly, a cake made of cornmeal and water with salt if available and baked on a hoe or shovel. I doubt it. Hoe, I'd guess, refers to the hod or low brick fender around a hearth. Indians and early Yankees used flat slates or soapstone for the same purpose.

11. Could you eat *rocktripe*?

In absolute desperation, yes. Rocktripe is a large lichen growing on forest rocks. Boiled long enough, it will sustain life, though it may not seem worth it because it can make you sick.

12. Would you serve the parson a *tardy*?

No. Not if he was expected. Tardy was another name for *hash*, made when someone came tardy to table or when the Old Woman was tardy herself: fried leftovers.

13. Would a dutiful wife give her husband a *squib*?

Indeed she would, and every night at that. A squib

(some places called it a *rising*) was a snack set out the night before to see the Old Man through chores. Any decent Yankee husband always rose first, started the fire, and only then headed for the barn. All he asked was that breakfast be ready when he got back. A squib would be a slab of pie, cold meat or a *hank* of well-buttered bread.

14. For what would you use *Holy Harry*?

Holy Harry! was one of a dozen names for hot peppers or of any sauce made therefrom. Not native to New England, though a fair substitute was made from buttercup seeds.

15. Did the Yankee housewife use many herbs for food?

No, most were medicinal, not culinary. Few if any were grown only for flavor; that is, for *bracing* food. The housewife's weak point was spices — principally nutmeg, cinnamon, ginger and cloves — but she'd claim each one had a *tonic* value as well. Didn't want to seem frivolous.

16. What were the commonest meats on the Yankee table?

In early times, game as often as possible (we'll come to that later). As noted, fish was not considered meat, only fish, although it virtually replaced meat in coastal regions. The commonest meats were pork and fowl, but the only year-round red meat was mutton or lamb. Fresh pork came only in killing season; all that was not made up into bacon and hams was put down in brine. *Salt pork* was not the same as sowbelly, which has no *streak* (lean) to it.

17. Was ham a Yankee favorite on the farm?

No, not if they raised it.

The ham's a long and loathesome toil,
Three days to freshen, two to boil,
A half-day's turning on the spit,
One sup — and that's the end of it...

I suspect that was mostly sour grapes: Most hams were sold; a prime whole ham, cured to perfection, could fetch more than half a dollar sometimes.

18. What was a *rasher* of bacon?

A good thick slice, seldom fried, never crisp or drained, but *tonged* or *rashered* over the open fire till properly limp if barely hot.

19. How might the Yankee housewife select a chicken for dinner?

All else being equal and all chickens being eligible for the honor, she might toss up a straw or twig and whatever bird it landed on was doomed. This notion well may go back to Druid times: It was their way of picking a human for sacrifice. (A great-great-grandmother of mine, rumor has it, used the same method to pick a husband out of a batch of suitors.)

12.

Switzel
& Adam's Ale

Refreshing Liquids

The Yankee's liquid adventures were by no means confined to cider. The great American passion for soft drinks is rooted in the Yankee imagination, primed by necessity and often by defiance: Conventional drinks were not merely in chancey supply but were outrageously taxed by the Crown and, later, by the states themselves.

Once you've mastered the answers to these, you'll have a batch of notions you may want to try yourself. No recipes are given. That's half the fun.

1. Would you offer a parson *Adam's ale*?

Yes, and likely little else. Adam's ale is a temperance term for water, the sufficient and innocent drink of Eden. It was also a common name for a good spring, flowing year round and open in winter.

2. Did Yankees make their own beer?

Indeed they did, as soon as enough land was cleared to grow the grain. They made no big thing of it, but beer, ale, stout and porter were as common as cider, and they were made, more often than not, at home. They also grew their own hops for *bitters*, a mildly alcoholic, bitter tonic.

3. Were they great coffee drinkers?

No. Coffee came late into New England. Even in England the coffeehouse was not known till well into the eighteenth century, contrary to most belief. The early Yankees' great addiction was tea.

4. What did they use for tea?

China tea, mostly; the Indian teas came a bit later. Green teas were known, but black teas were preferred. Yankee teas were by no means restricted to imported versions. Dried raspberry leaves made a fair substitute, as did a dozen teas made from herbs. Wintergreen, both berries and leaves, were free for the taking and thought healthful as well as refreshing, as were young willow shoots or bark, one of many bracers. Sassafras was most highly touted of all, long thought to be a true panacea, a "cure-all."

5.   What substitutes did they use for coffee?

The roots of chickory ("cornflower") and dandelion, dried and ground, to which might be added blanched acorns and parched barley, the whole roasted. *Malted* (sprouted) barley, well dried, was also added.

6.   What was *mead*?

Once common in New England, it is one of man's oldest drinks, probably predating wine. It's made from fermented honey. One old Vermonter claimed he made it better from maple syrup.

7.   What was a *parson's passion*?

Tea with both cream and sugar. One tale has it that it was always served to a candidate parson. If he took his tea with both, he was judged too passionate for the job — too high a liver.

8.   Did old-time Yankees make wine?

Yes, not always from grapes. Apple wine was made cutting off the "working" of cider when it was short of "hard." Elderberry and dandelion wine were the great favorites and not included in Temperance proscription, being considered *tonics*. Fine wines were imported to grace the gentry's tables, but little trickled down to the common Yankee. He got by: All those ancient grapevines you find were not there just for jelly.

9.   Just what was a *teetotaler*?

An Abstainer in private, a Prohibitionist in public, a nuisance in general, not merely to breweries and saloon-keepers. His toughest opposition came from factory and mill owners, whose company-owned saloons took back most of their workers' pay, sometimes before they were even out the gate.

10. Did teetotalers drink only tea?

Not by a long shot. They were the instigators and often the inventors of "soft" drinks. (See below.) (The *tee* in teetotaler, by the way, has nothing to do with tea. It's just an added emphasis for the word *total*.)

11. Why were soft drinks called *dopes* in New England?

Because that's what they often contained. Lithium was originally used in 7-Up, cocaine was an ingredient of early Coca-Cola, and caffeine still is in it and in other such commercial drinks. But not a drop of alcohol, by gum!

12. What was *switzel*?

Sometimes called *swizzle*, occasionally miscalled *sprill*, most commonly *harvest drink* or *harvester*, it was a concoction of vinegar, molasses or brown sugar; pure, cold springwater; and whatever else you might care to add in the way of spice — ginger, cinnamon or nutmeg, or a handful of crushed mint. Made up by the gallons for harvest hands, particularly during haying. Right bracey!

13.

Ox Gall
& Onion Candy

Yankee Medicine Chest

If winter and work, Puritans and Indians didn't do the old-time Yankee in, he still had another hurdle to go: surviving the state of medicine. Distrustful of what was, by comparison, a fairly enlightened profession in New England, Yankees mainly relied on their own notions and potions, concocted from whatever *materia medica* they could lay their hands on — most of it growing right around them. While I don't necessarily recommend any of the nostrums mentioned here, there was very little quackery and a good measure of reason in Yankee medicine — enough, at least, to be borrowed in some instances by modern pharmacology, though usually without giving too much credit to the source.

1. Why did medicine always taste so horrible?

Some believed that the worse the taste, the greater the effect. Perfectly lovely concoctions, like cherried honey, would be bittered up or soured down. Perhaps the idea was to discourage malingering. But since many medicines were close to two-hundred-proof alcohol, it may have been to discourage random doses by non-invalids.

2. Why would a Yankee call in the barber instead of the doctor?

For bloodletting (which is what the red stands for on a barberpole) and for most minor surgery. The doctor practiced *medicine*; *cutting* was beneath him. Even if he prescribed bloodletting, he would pass the job on to the barber if possible. (This dichotomy still exists between internists and surgeons.)

3. Did early doctors do housecalls?

In remoter parts, that was *all* they made. Some, like preachers, rode circuit.

4. How did people protect children from measles?

By putting them to bed with a child who had come down with measles. It was believed that the sooner they got it over with, the better. Some also held that contagion lessened severity — four kids with measles meant that each would have it only one-quarter as hard, there being only so many measles to go around.

5.   Why did old-time Yankee mothers keep a jar of cobwebs handy?

For stopping nosebleeds. Works every time!

6.   What was *asafoetida* famous for?

Just about everything, but mainly for its stink. Imported from China — it is a gum derived from an Oriental plant — it was put in a sachet and hung around the neck. It appeared to reduce epidemic diseases in kids, probably by keeping the wearer at a good distance and so reducing contagion.

7.   Why did druggists keep a jar of live leeches?

For bleeding people. Simpler, more sanitary, and cheaper than calling in the barber.

8.   For two stumps each, name three old cures for the common cold.

Saleratus and water; ginger tea (hot milk, lots of sugar and as much ginger as you can stand); mustard poultice (paste) on your chest, covered with red flannel; mustard footbath; mustard and honey; *nitre* and warm water (nitre is potassium nitrate or saltpeter, thus should be avoided by bridegrooms); a hearty pinch of gunpowder (which contains not only saltpeter but sulphur and charcoal); hot rum with nutmeg (worth catching a cold for); pumpkin water (water pumpkin has been boiled in); raw onion in vinegar... and so on. There are thousands all told, at least a hundred of which I've tried.

9.   What was the cure for a sore throat?

There were almost as many cures as for the general cold, but the best of all was cherry syrup and honey. Most effective was onion candy. Sounds odd but this is one that should be tried: Slice an onion very thinly, spread out on an old plate, sprinkle with sugar, and set on the back of the stove (or low oven) till candied.

10. What was the standard *spring tonic* for kids?

Sulphur and molasses, given whether you were peaked or *peakit* (wan, pale, listless) or not. Proportions varied but the taste was the same: ghastly.

11. If you got migraine, what was certain to follow?

Baldness. It worked in reverse, too. Baldness brought on migraines. Ladies used lavender tea; gentlemen ate onions or garlic; myrtle leaf tea, well boiled down, also worked — at least on the migraine. For baldness, try rosemary tea, *very* strong.

12. What was a *clyster*?

Now a Yankee Unmentionable, it was a nutritious enema: When the patient couldn't be fed at one end, he was fed at the other. Sounds gross, but this was in the days before intravenous feeding had come along. Broth, warm milk and, *in extremis*, rum or whiskey or other liquid medicines were used.

13. What was ox gall used for?

Yankeedom's version of Ex-Lax. Gall was dried and portioned out as needed, very sparingly. Any animal's gall worked, but ox was preferred. The ox, being the most powerful animal, supposedly had the strongest gall. Gall, by the way, is the bitterest natural substance known.

14. What was *camomile* tea used for?

Cured neuralgia, asthma, common and uncommon colds. It was a general *stomacher*, tonic, and bracer; reduced fever; induced fever; excellent for cherking up folks with rheumatism; helped with shingles, chilblains and earache; cleared stuffy noses; promoted healing and general well-being. And if it didn't work, you could always try tansy, catnip or pennyroyal, if you lacked sassafras.

15. How might you treat chapped hands on the farm?

Mutton (sheep) tallow mixed with the balm of the balsam poplar (*balm of Gilead*). A trash tree of generally no use to anything but woodpeckers, its leaf-buds produce a strongly scented, sticky balm.

16. Were many older-time Yankees "dope addicts"?

The use of laudanum, an opium derivitive, was common to ease pain and induce rest and sleep. Thanks to the Clipper trade, New England had ready access to opium from Indochina. The lovely poppies that spring up around old New England houses were originally planted for a home-grown source, but few Yankees had the skill or patience to produce it. Heroin was widely used in patent medicines and, of itself, boasted as a safe cubstitute for opium (from which heroin comes). None were controlled until the first decades of this century. Paregoric, also from opium, was widely used, especially for teething babies — or wakeful ones. Cocaine, first brought in as baled leaf, was useful in the slave trade and for some slave owners, who hoped originally to reduce slave rations, since it assuages hunger. As mentioned, its use in commercial soft drinks continued well into this century. But possibly the oddest rage in "substances" was nitrous oxide or *laughing gas*. Used first by dentists and some surgeons as an anesthetic, it quickly became fashionable to hold *gas parties*. It really did make you laugh, by the way, and act generally giddy.

14.

Pokes & Buskins

Yankee Attire

It wasn't just an inbred distaste for the frivolous and sumpjus that máde the ordinary Yankee a plain dresser. It was simple economics. Scarcity of both goods and the money to buy them left the Yankee to his or her own devices. Fine clothes were saved for Sunday and to be married and buried in. A man might go a lifetime with a single suit, a woman with one gown, and many went without either. The Yankee woman was clever-fingered and made do as marvelously with her thimble as with her cookpot.

1.   Why were there fringes on buckskins?

These were not for decoration at all. The purpose was to *runnel* off the rain faster. They were also handy spare lacings and for patchings when loading a gun.

2. Where did the Yankee get his clothes?

In the boondocks, from what he raised or shot. Linen from flax and wool from sheep were the two mainstays, augmented by leather and buckskin and some — but little — fur. Cotton was expensive until well into the eighteenth century.

3. What were *buskins*?

Boots or shoes with extra leather to their uppers, often coming to the knee, where they might be turned down in swashbuckley folds.

4. How did Yankees negotiate mudpuddles?

No one on earth has more expertise about mud than a Yankee, for obvious reasons. Sheep tallow and lard and suet were all used to keep shoes somewhat waterproof, but mud demanded *pattens*, usually of wood with two- or three-inch cleats on the bottom. These were slipped on over shoes and strapped in place, removed when back on dry land again.

5. What was *linsey-woolsey*?

Linen and wool woven together, mainly woolen yarn woven on a linen warp, though sometimes spun together for both woof and warp. The basic old-time cloth for coats, britches and other everyday wear.

6.   How old must a boy be to get britches?

Real britches — long ones, that is, didn't happen till he had his full growth or near to it. He might get them a few years sooner but they'd have to be let down as needed. Knee pants were the rule through boyhood, though knickers were common in later times. A child, whether a boy or girl, stayed in dresses till three.

7.   *What was a tricorn?*

The much-touted three-cornered hat of the Revolutionary Yankee (and others) was really a round hat with a very wide round brim — wide enough to act as a partial umbrella if one hunched hard enough. It could also be tied down around the ears. Some parsons held the tricorn as a symbol of the Trinity — at least till they turned Unitarian. Parsons and Quakers often wore them rolled up only on the sides. (See your old Quaker Oats box!) *Pitmen* — sawyers at the lower end of a pit saw — stitched on extra brimming to ward off the sawdust showering down on them.

8.   What were corsets made out of?

Corsets or *stays* had as their vital ingredient *whalebone*, which wasn't bone at all, but the *baleen* of whales' mouths, a sort of super-sized soup strainer. Baleen, for a time, was almost as important a product as whale oil.

9.   Did Yankee women wear corsets?

Not much except perhaps for Sundays. It impeded honest labor. Besides, corsets came dear.

10. Why were aprons so important to Yankee housewives?

For protecting their *gooder* clothes, of course. But a quick change took place when company hove into view: Women always kept a *company apron* on a peg in the kitchen to rush into as needed.

11. What was a *tuck*?

Aprons used to be large and near to floor-length. They could be *hiked up* into a double fold, a tuck at the waist, which made a dandy pocket. (I've seen a baby slung in one!)

12. Did most Yankee women wear *farthingales*?

No. Farthingales were very wide hooped skirts, just stuff and nonsense to Yankee women, fit only for the upper gentry's ladies at fancy balls.

13. What part of their bodies were Yankees most proud of?

Their waists. Uncommonly proud — though you'd never know it today. A man might boast that he "ain't let out a stitch since twenty..."; and girls considered sixteen inches at the waist to be just about right, though eighteen was permitted. But before you despair, remember these eighteenth- and nineteenth-century Yankees, like most other humans, were much shorter and generally smaller: Five-foot-six was a good-sized man, and many girls called it quits when they'd reached five feet even. (George Washington's biggest asset may have been that he was well over six feet — a veritable giant of a man.)

14. When did Yankee ladies wear gloves?

Gloves were an absolute must for church and higher social callings, and a pair would be treasured for years. Some, delicately stitched and made of kidskin, might set one back the better part of a dollar just for a pair. Ladies *tatted* their own if they had to. But gloves were never worn for warmth. Mittens were the rule and, when dressed up, a muff.

15. What was *tawdry*?

The word is derived from St. Audrey, who wore fine things to celebrate her faith. This naturally set a fashion, but women who couldn't buy real finery were supplied with cheap imitations, particularly of lace. Tawdry, which we know now as a derogatory word, to early Yankee women simply meant *store-boughten*, especially lace or other *frillery*. So she'd add a *touch of tawdry* to fancy-up otherwise plain dresses. She also tatted her own lace, by the way.

16. What was used for dye in the old days?

About the only commercial dye was indigo, and it was both scarce and expensive, even though much was grown and made in America. But, as usual, the Yankee women made do. Some *woad*, which yielded a dull blue, was grown; more was brought over from England. Butternut gave her the *Quaker grey*, goldenrod and other plants provided yellows and reds. But the most beautiful shades of all came from lichens: pinks, violets, lavenders, warm russets and colors that haven't a proper name. (One lady I know has recovered more than two hundred natural dyes from the Yankee past!)

17. You wouldn't take home *a pig in a poke*, of course, but might you go for a *girl in a poke*?

To buy a pig in a poke, of course, meant to buy sight unseen, which Yankees never did (though a slicker at a fair might switch a cat for a new-bought shoat; when the farmer got home, he *let the cat out of the bag* — discovered the awful truth). But a girl in a poke was a different matter entirely. With the advent of larger-scale commercial milling, the sacks meal came in were a source of *pokecloth*. (Poke was cotton finely woven; *sack* (as in sackcloth) was coarse jute or burlap.) Milling companies capitalized on this by making sacks of bright prints, with the mill's name and other data printed in washable inks. Girls collected enough pokes to make up a dress. One form of girls' party was a *poke-swap*, getting together to trade around unwanted prints from their *pokestashes*. Going to town, they carried *snips* (swatches) of desired prints to match at the feedstore.

And from all this: to be *pokey* is not to be slow, as in slowpoke, just countrified and maybe a bit shy and, oftener than not, *pretty as a poke*. Such girls made fine wives, demanding little and able to make do and, for some reason, generally truer as sweethearts, even if you had to go *back in the pokes* (boondocks) to find one. Go try it.

15.

Frolicks
& Spousies

The Art of Keeping Warm

The new, well-heeled brand of country living named the Good Life has bred a clutter of experts who talk endlessly about BTUs, R-Factors and the relative merits of hundred-dollar firewood and thousand-dollar stoves. Take away their urethane cocoons and they'd disappear down the pike in their Volvos, whipped before Christmas. The following questions, if you know the answers, will save you from ever being beguiled by these winterhaters, who don't know a *muffle* from a *spinster's spouse*, and can't tell a *basker* from a *heelstone*.

1.   Name the best way to keep from getting cold feet.

Shake some pepper into your socks. The irritation keeps the blood perking down there.

2.   Why did wool longjohns work best?

For the same reason. They'd itch your whole skin up into a positive fever. By the time spring came, you'd almost miss the agony.

3.   What's a *potato-pocket*?

A pocket with a potato in it, usually one on each side. Baked in the ashes overnight, the potatoes were raked out in the morning and popped into coat pockets to keep your hands warm for the long trek to school where, rewarmed on the schoolhouse stove, they could be eaten for lunch. When the weather was *pockets both ways*, it was as cold at the day's end as it had been at the start. Woodcutters, hunters and trappers used potatoes, also.

4.   Would you keep a meal hot in a *warming pan*?

A *warming pan* was a tightly covered brass pan with a very long handle. Filled with coals, it was slipped under the bedcovers between the icy sheets and moved round and round to warm them. Sometimes called a *bedpan* in the old days, and wrongly called a *frolick* (see below). For pity's sake, be sure the lid's snapped tight, and keep the thing moving.

5.   How could you break your toe in bed?

Aside from your spouse, the most dangerous item in bed would be a *heelstone*: a brick or more often a slab of soapstone, warmed up good by the fire, wrapped in flannel and tucked into the bottom of the bed to keep your feet warm. Kick around too much and you wound up with a broken toe or two.

6.   Would you use a frolick in your bed?

No, though it was second cousin to the warming pan. It was a small iron box filled with coals for taking along to church or on a journey to keep your feet from freezing. Only elder females deigned to use them, younger ones having their own methods (see below).

7.   What was the pleasantest way to keep warm?

Bundling, which was invented in New England and swiped by the Pennsylvania Dutch, who now take credit for it. At times and certain places, it was considered a perfectly acceptable form of courting, the couple being tucked into the cold corner of the room, and the hearthside thus saved for others. It was somewhat frowned on when undertaken out of sight of parents, where *muffling* was preferred: That's bundling in two bundles instead of one. But then, there always were the lap robes of sleighs and buggies, in which instance the couple was *buffaling*.

8.   Would you do your *flouncies* in front of callers?

I should hope not! This was hiking up your skirts to the fireplace to warm your *unders*. Risky, but a mighty comfort.

9. If you were given some *yargles,* what might you do with them?

Wear 'em, be glad you got 'em, and hope you'll get enought to get *all yargled up* for the winter. Possibly the word's from *argyle* (as in argyle socks) and meant heavy knitwear; hence, any warm winter clothing.

10. Why was the hired man often the warmest in winter?

He was usually kept in the barn, over the stable, and had the benefit of animal heat rising under him, plus the heat from the manure pile under the stable, plus no end of hay on all sides and above him.

11. What was a *bellybanner?*

More politely called a *sursingle*, it was a wide strip of cloth, red flannel if possible, wound around one's middle, warming that least-warmable and always-complaining part, the small of the back. They should be revived!

12. How might a woodcutter keep warm?

By building a *basker* or *hasty*, a lean-to made of brush from his cutting, with more brush piled up in front to feed a good strong fire. Not that a Yankee woodcutter ever

needed a basker for himself, understand. It was just to draw
the frost from the axes.

13. Where in the bed did the smallest child go in the winter?

Smack-dab in the middle of his brothers and sisters.
And if there wasn't room in the bed the long way, have 'em
sleep across it the short way, *all* of 'em.

14. And what, pray tell, kept a spinster warm?

A *spinster's spouse*, which was a long bolster of wool
in a flannel cover, warmed up before the fire and taken to
bed with her. Warmed her head to toe and doubtless aided
her dreams. But *spousies* weren't just for spinsters. There
was often one for each family member.

15. What does *putting your feet in the oven* mean?

It means putting your feet in the oven. A standard
treatment, especially for small, cold boys. One of the
warmest wintertime greetings was, "Well, pity's sake! Pull
up a chair and stick 'em in!"

16. What might a body use to keep warm at night if all else fails?

Cats. Cheap, warm, durable and moderately dependable. And, I suspect, used far more than admitted at present. I've known foot-cats and back-cats, belly-cats, shoulder specialists, purrers, yawners, stretchers and treaders and wakers. A well-trained cat will stay wherever you place her the night long, never budging a whisker. How one trains a cat, however, is another matter.

16.

Kalpies & Clattershanks

The Supernatural

New England may well be the pool from which most other American ghoulies crawl. There isn't a corner of the region that hasn't its own version of the Walking Lady or the Devil's Bride; each sea town has its share of ghost ships, of wave walkers, of how sea change overcame some mortal man. And the memory of witches is still strong enough to raise suspicions now and then. So here are a few matters it might be well to know about before you come face to face with one of them, as you doubtless will.

1.   Who was *Himself?*

Why, that's the Devil Himself, of course! It was considered unwise to ever name him outright, since he'd answer promptly to Satan, Lucifer, Old Nick, Beelzebub, and the rest, while Himself might confuse him — for a time.

2.   What was the difference between *incubus* and *succubus?*

Sex. The first was male, the second female, and thus roughly on a par with *warlock* and *witch*. However, they might change genders at will, so you couldn't tell which was witch, you might say. Some held that an incubus forced otherwise blameless females to become witches, while a succubus did the same to equally flawless lads.

3.   How many witches were burned in America?

None at all, in America. They were all hanged but one; he was pressed to death under stones. Some unofficial executions in Connecticut and Rhode Island, legend has it, were brought off simply by tying the poor wretches to stakes at low water and letting the rising tide do the work.

4.   How might you tell a witch?

Short of catching one red-handed on her broomstick, it's not easy, but there are several ways to go at it. Tell her sad, sad tales: No witch can weep. Hold her under water an hour; if she drowns, she wasn't a witch after all. Perhaps the surest clue is the eye: Witches have cold, hard, uncaring stares, however much they may smile — somewhat like bankers. A silver spoonful of baby tears dashed in their faces makes them scream. They passionately dislike garlic, but adore the gall of a rooster, offered raw. A cat set down near a suspected witch will lick its fur backwards. In all, it's best not to look too close in the first place.

5.   Why would you put rue on a coffin?

Some say rue, some use tansy, others claim that St. Johnswort will do it best. But a sprig of it dropped on the coffinlid once it's been lowered into the grave — but never, never sooner! — will keep the soul of the coffin's tenant from rising and walking the nights about.

6.   Did Yankees believe in *banshees*?

Yes. Many did, and some still may. Banshees are not exclusively Irish. Many people believed in a *keener*, whose scream announced a death just before the event. A *boreen* (which I've heard as well as heard of) acted much the same, but its cry is more like a whimper. If such things keep on screaming after the death, it should be taken as a good sign that the Devil hasn't gotten the soul — yet.

7.   Might you take a ride on a *kalpie*?

Yes, but only once. Kalpies are horse-like horribles from the sea, made of scud and wrack and flying foam cast up on beaches in the night. They'll rise up and come inland to graze in the watermeadows, enticing you to mount. But once you're up, they'll bolt for the sea and carry you to your doom with 'em. Some used to say they're the ghosts of horses jettisoned at sea by ships in distress needing to lighten load.

8. What was (and perhaps still is) a *wave walker*?

These are the shades of drowned fishermen and sailors, walking the waves back to their homes. They appear most often in still, bitter, winter weather when the water puts up little puffs of dense mist called *sea smoke*. Sadly, the wave walkers never quite reach shore, dissolving and sinking almost within grasp of dry land.

9. When would you use a *cooling board*?

A corpse was laid out and *rivened up* (made ready) for the coffin on a plank, sometimes improvised from a door, sometimes made special and kept in the attic for just that purpose. Kids used to dare each other to lie down on it. One crazy old lady used a cooling board for a bed, to save bother, she said, should she die in the night. Which, as a matter of fact, she did, but it took twenty years.

10. How might your child be born *marked*?

It was long believed — and for all I know still is —that a fright or surprise of the mother while she was pregnant could leave its mark on the unborn. The sight of a three-legged cat, for example, and the child would be born lame; meet a hunchback and the child would be lucky; too close to a bolt of lightning could strike it blind. Eating too many strawberries would put a "strawberry" (a small red birthmark) on the baby's skin forever; to be caught in a thunderstorm bred an ill temper; while the merest glimpse of Himself gave the child a tail.

11. How could folks tell the Devil had paid you a visit?

By the state of your hair, especially on waking. Knots, snarls, and kinks were absolute evidence you'd been planning Evil or dreaming of Sin. Though some more kindly people called these merely *elfknots*, True Christians knew better. One poor little lad I knew had his head shaved clean by his granny, that neighbors might never guess what went on inside. But his hair grew back with horns where there'd only been cowlicks — proof that Himself had taken up permanent residence inside.

12. What were *spiggans*, and what might you do about 'em?

Also known as *spriggans*, *spraygarns* or *spagoons*, the only adjective for them is hideous, and to make matters worse they're proud of it, it seems, making themselves visible in full daylight to anyone with so much as a drop of Irish or West Scots blood in them. There is no avoiding them, no remedy against them, and sooner or later they're going to get you — and, believe me, you'll know it when they do!

13. Can you really silence a *presence*?

No, for they're silent already, never making a sound, never letting you even glimpse them. They're *felt*. Step into an empty room and discover that it isn't really empty at all —that's a *presence*. For the most part, they're merely watchers and listeners, though sometimes they'll exude a slight chill of reproof around you. But they come on strongly enough to stop your feet in their tracks, prickle your hackles, and cock your ears. Whisper a name and they'll sometimes leave — if you know the right name to whisper. In my own old house, I use *Lavinia* or *Letitia* or *Abigail* (d. 1767, 1792 and 1821, respectively).

14. What were *toosoontooks*?

These are the saddest of all shades, by any reckoning: the spirits of children. They appear — often clearly — to living children, asking to play with them or begging a bit of candy. The name is mistaken for some Indian word, but it's English entire: children took off too soon. And many were: one graveyard (near my house), now overgrown with cedar and juniper, held seven little stones in a row, the eldest eleven, the youngest not yet a year, all "took off" within a dozen days, probably by diptheria.

15. Did *exorcism* always work?

Not by a long shot. Bell, book and candle, prayer said backwards, sweepings with willow brooms, even fumigation with sassafras or garlic could never be counted on absolutely — and still can't be. One old man in Rhode Island, exhausted by the shades and presences infecting his house, in desperation burned it to the ground and built a brand new house on its foundations. Back they came, the first night he moved in, all trooping up the cellar stairs. So you see it's wisest not to even try to be rid of such things. In a way, it isn't fair. After all, they've been in residence a whole lot longer than *you* have.

16. What is the *Axeman* always looking for?

Now this isn't a collection of ghost stories, of course, so such things as the *Gold-Clew* and *Annie Grimes*, the *Silligo Man*, the *Beggartrap* and the truth of the *Bride of Briderock* I'll tell you about some other time. But the Axeman you've probably heard about yourself, told in a dozen ways and a score of places. Remember? *He's* the one you hear chopping, chopping, chopping in the woods on winter nights. He's out trying to find the wife he stuffed into a hollow tree when she complained of a lack of firewood. When he went back to fetch her home, he couldn't find the tree — and he still hasn't.

17. Who — or what — is *Old Clattershanks*?

You may know him by some other name, but the sound is always the same: the rattle of bones being shaken in a bag — a sort of dull chinking. Old Clattershanks will always be behind you. Spin around quick as you may, he'll still be behind you — and catching up, to boot. Some say of course that it's only the sound the wind makes through tree branches after an icestorm. But why, then, is he to be heard as often in summer?

17.

Luckers
& Loveknots

The Superstitious

Old Yankees drew a clear line between the supernatural and the superstitious. Every one might agree, for instance, that ghoulies (ghosts, spirits) do exist. But how one dealt with them was a matter of personal opinion. Each Yankee had his or her own *warders*, objects or acts to ward off evil or contrary fortune, and lifelong argument often resulted. So, to avoid controversy and disappointment, I've included here only those that *really* work. Try 'em and see.

1.   What were *luckers*, black and white?

Truly prepared small boys always carried both kinds of *luckers* or *lucky stones*, black for day, white for night, one in each pocket, and don't ever let 'em touch! Any lucker had to be small, smooth and the rounder the luckier, but marbles didn't count. Rub the white one for luck; the black to avoid bad luck. Infallible, but not to be used against ghoulies (see below).

2.   If ghoulies were after you, what could you do besides run? (Name at least three.)

Hide your thumbs in your fists. Most ghoulies grab their victims by their thumbs, you know.

Toss crumbs behind you; pebbles in a pinch, but cookie crumbs work best.

Sprinkle salt in your shoes before venturing out on a ghoulie kind of night. If you don't have shoes, rub salt on your heels.

Walk backwards. Since ghoulies always walk behind you, this way they'll have to walk backwards, too, which they dread to do, for fear of tripping back into their graves.

Lead them under a witch-hazel bush.

Crow like a rooster. They might think it's morning and scuttle back to their graves.

3.   What was a *poke-penny*?

Poke-pennies were to girls what luckers were to boys. They must never be carried but sewn into your dress somewhere. Girls being luckier than boys, you only needed one.

4.   What happens to girls who whistle?

Nothing good. You'd be baiting the Devil. Start as a tomboy, you'll later be a *reckless maid*, and the town will be whispering after you:

Whistlin' girls an' crowin' hens
Are sure to come to no good ends;
One difference betwixt the twa:
A crowin' hen will never lay...

5.   Might you whistle in the kitchen?

You know better than to even ask! It will sour good milk, keep bread from rising and "work" the freshest cider. Only the kettle's allowed to whistle there!

6.   If you find a pin, why should you pick it up?

So "all the day, you'll have good luck..." Pins were once rare and precious things, each being made by hand. A wife sold eggs and butter to gain herself *pin money* for notions and trifles, buttons and bows, threads and needles — and pins. So finding one was luck in itself.

7.   If you lose your britches-button, what does it mean? And what on earth can you do?

It means the Devil is loosing your britches to flail you good or make you trip when they drop. (Boys' britches were held up by a single "brace" over the shoulder and secured by a single button, so its loss could be a disaster.) Besides holding your britches up with your fist until you got home, the only cure was to toss a stone behind you. Go back and find it — and you'll find your button, too.

8.   Did horseshoes bring good luck?

Yes, but only if nailed up with the toe down, to keep the luck from spilling out. Oxbows were sometimes used, too, but weren't as lucky. (The game of horseshoes, by the way, was sometimes called *chuck-a-luck*; you'd get few *ringers*, however, if you didn't know where, when, and how to spit on the shoe you were tossing.)

9.   Why would you wear a feather in your cap?

In early times Yankees wore them in defiance of the sumptuary laws and Puritan ordinances which forbade such *flummery*. Gravediggers wore them in defiance of the reason for their trade. (One I know in Vermont still does.) And that most defiant of all Yankees, Doodle himself, you'll remember, "stuck a feather in his hat and called it maca-roni..." (And while we're at it, a *macaroni* was "a traveled young man who affected foreign ways," according to Webster.) Indians, of course, used feathers far more seri-ously: as hard-earned merit badges. With Yankees, their use was mostly satirical.

10.   Why did Indians throw tobacco on ash trees?

To propitiate the tree's spirit, a handful of tobacco was strewn on the roots when the Indian took wood from the tree for a bow. The tree itself was never cut, the strip for the bow being chiseled out of its living trunk.

11.   When should corn be planted?

In olden times, not until oak leaves are as big as a mouse's ear. Some Yankees had a specific tree for this, which they also considered lucky for kissing under.

12. What should you plant in the dark of the moon? And what, when the moon is full?

"Plant in the dark what grows in the dark; plant in the full what grows in the light." Thus potatoes, turnips, carrots, onions, and the like must be planted when the moon is "under." Corn, peas, beans, cabbage and the like, only when the moon is full.

13. Over which shoulder should you see the evening star when you make a wish?

Over your left, of course, left being closest to the heart. You can see it over your right, but your wish won't come true.

14. What might a buttercup tell a girl?

Whether she'll grow up fat or lean. Hold the blossom under your chin. If it reflects its butter color on your skin, you're bound to grow up chubby.

15. To whom would you first tell family news?

To the cows and to the bees. Deaths, births, troths (engagements), homecomings or leavings should first be whispered into bossy's ear, or whispered into the hive. This notion seems to have come from the West Country of England and from Ireland and may have to do with the

Biblical milk and honey. At least there's an old nursery rhyme:

> *Fiddle-de-dee, fiddle-de-dee!*
> *In Goshen-land we all will be*
> *When the cow has married the bumble-bee...*

16. And speaking of bees: What should you do when you see one sleeping?

Grind your scythe and whet your sickle. As goeth one old couplet:

> *Corn's ripe for reaping*
> *When bees are sleeping...*

Corn here refers to grain, not maize, which is Indian corn. In late summer the nectar of flowers may ferment and the bee gets tipsy from it, becoming not a bumble but a stumble-bee. So there may be a drop of sense in this superstition.

17. How would you make a *loveknot*?

From the hair of your lover. If he's not your lover yet, a thread from his coat will do, but it must be stolen. Lovers used to exchange *lock-chains*, bracelets of hair, his made from hers, hers from his, sometimes boldly mingled. Never trust such things to work with sailors, however. They boasted a dozen varieties of loveknots, many of which would unravel completely at a single tug.

18. What should lie under the mast of every ship?

A coin. Silver brings longer luck than gold.

19. Would you have a black cat on your ship?

Yes indeed. No ship was complete without its cat, even black, to keep the rats at bay. The best of all was a tortoiseshell cat or a callico, by which any sensible mariner foretold the weather just by the lay of its fur.

20. Step on a *pissmire* and what will happen?

The same as will happen if you step on a spider or a beetle: It'll rain, every time. Just wait and see! Pissmire is a Yankee word for ant.

21. If your ears ring, what does it mean?

There's gossip abroad about you. If the left ear rings, they're saying ill of you; if the right, they're singing your praises.

22. What do you first put in the hole when you're planting an orchard tree?

An egg. Actually, this is a great economy. In the very, very olden days (well predating New England), they used a virgin.

23. Should you toss your hat on a bed?

Never! It will bring ruin to whoever sleeps in the bed, and worse ruin to yourself. You shouldn't even bring a hat into a bedroom.

24. Should you thank someone who gave you an aspidistra?

Never! You'll kill it. Any houseplant that's thanked for is doomed. The same for herbs or any rooted plant. Slips may be thanked for, but it's still risky.

25. If a woman wants a child, how should she wear her hair?

Each night, over the left shoulder and in front. However, this is not guaranteed to work in reverse — right shoulder for no children.

26. And if she wants the child to be a boy?

All babes in the womb are girls *unless*: You button your shoes when you take them off; don't look at the moon when it's new; go pat your grandmother's knee (or tombstone); pick no daisy, touch no tansy, pet no cat in the daylight; and if all this fails, simply try again...

18.

Round Heels
& Buggydusters

Love and Marriage

Love was a mighty serious game with the old Yankees; maybe still is. Resources were limited, means simple, rules exacting, and there were always at least four umpires for every two players. But, as with any other pursuit, Yankees made do with what was at hand. It must have worked somehow: There never was any shortage of little Yankees.

1. Casting about for a mate, would you *pick a mayflower?*

117

Yes, indeed, but it wouldn't mean a descendant of Puritans. *Going mayflowering* — looking for arbutus, that earliest and most fragrant of all wildflowers — was the best Rite of Spring. Now and then a girl came home with a mite more than mayflowers for the day's work, which led to a *mayflower wedding.*

2.   If a girl got *heiffery* on you, would you curl her toes?

If your girl went *heiffery* on you — got passionate, you might say — then the least you could do was to enter into the spirit of the occasion and make the poor thing's *toes curl.* But, often as not, she wouldn't even let you try. Nothing's more *baity* than a heiffered-up girl who gets you all *hackled,* only to heed her mother's admonition: "Now, Sally, you see to it that you *keep your toes straight!*"

3.   Would you hanker after a girl who had *round heels?*

Probably, but not permanently. This affliction — some say it ran in whole families — meant that a girl had consistent trouble in remaining upright and could be tipped over without much of a push. She had, they'd say, "more'n one spoon in her cup and all of 'em stirrin'," or "she's seen more sky than grass."

4.   What was a *courting door?*

A *courting door* usually led to the back parlor and had holes cut in its top panels (in my old house they're heartshaped) so that *goings-on* inside the room might be peeked at. Otherwise, the couple within were free to do some truly serious courting.

5. How might you make a *two-headed buffalo?*

By you and your girl cuddling up under one buffalo robe, usually in a sleigh or pung. Before wind-chill factors got invented, this was a fine sport all winter. One couple out *punging* was described by an old gossip: "Durndest thing I ever did see! A horse being chased by an eight-legged buffalo!"

6. How was going for a *buggyride* dangerous?

Straight-laced parents frowned on buggyriding since the buggy could be parked. So to get *took for a buggyride* meant an untimely if necessary wedding. But the gravest danger of the buggyride was what it signified to those town gossips who "had their tongues hinged in the middle and wagging at both ends." If your girl waited for you to hand her out, that could only mean that things were serious. If she leapt over the wheel before you could hustle around to her side, why, then, the whole town knew her temper toward you. Another danger was that a horse, unlike a car, doesn't take constant steering. He'll just ploff along in whatever direction you point him, but he may not always heed shoulders and ditches. So if you ditched or *pitched* your buggy, the whole town knew your hands had been engaged somewhere other than on the reins.

7. Would it be a bad thing if, after you

dusted the buggy, you got *spruced from bit to crupper?*

Not at all. To *dust the buggy*, literally, was to get it ready in hope of conveying something better than oats and groceries. But to be *just buggydusting* meant being merely generally hopeful and in a high state of readiness. Things weren't earnest till the lad got himself, the horse, the harness *and* the buggy spruced up from bit to crupper (bit being the frontest part of the harness, crupper being the hindest). The girl might say that the boy didn't know bit from crupper about courting, but then he could say she wasn't worth dusting the buggy for, anyway.

8.   Would you marry a *Lydia Pinkham?*

Not if you knew she was one. The term comes from a famous "female complaint" tonic. Hence (to unsympathetic male chauvinists) any complaining woman. To be whined at was to be *fed a dose of Lydia Pinkham;* to have to put up with more of the same was to *swaller a bucket of moon balm.*

9.   In the real old days, would you want a *gossip* for a wife?

Indeed you would — in the original sense of this poor word. A *gossip* was any housewife. Before that, it meant the one person in the world closest to you, a God-friend (from Old English *God-sib*). Wives were regularly addressed as Gossip Brown, Gossip Smith, and so on, instead of *Mrs.* For husbands, the preferred term was *goodman, Mr.* being reserved for the gentry, *master* for young male children.

10. Would you fancy a *buxom* bride?

Absolutely, and not because she was full-bosomed. Like gossip, *buxom* is another plundered word. It has come to mean overblown, just plain fat ("she's a fine woman but a mite buxom "), or top-heavy. Originally, the word encompassed all that was good: healthy, robust, strong, rosy, jolly, cheerful, gay, willing, even-tempered, warm and happy. Lucky the man who landed a buxom bride! It meant obedient, too.

11. Might a Yankee maiden *swoon* if you *plighted* your *troth*?

No. Yankee lasses were never great swooners, even when a troth got plighted at them — that is, when the suitor pleaded his faithfulness: proposed. The swoon was more often caused by tight whalebones. Swooning or smelling salts — ammonia with a dash of perfume, perhaps — were used mainly by maiden ladies or by girls too fashionable to be worth proposing to anyway.

12. Could you *juld* a girl before you two were *spoke*?

No. A boy couldn't juld (jilt) a girl unless their *banns* had been "spoke" — announcement of their pending marriage "cried" from the pulpit. But a girl could be *jullied*, sort of just dropped away from. (She in turn could claim she'd disdained him.) No harm, unless the lass had been sullied, too. But either way, the boy mightn't care to keep living in the same town.

13. Did Yankees practice *primogeniture*?

Yes, at least some of them did. Primogeniture may sound like a sin, but it was only a bad habit, left over from English custom, of leaving all property to the first-born son. As one old rhyme has it:

> *First to the land,*
> *Next to the war,*
> *Third to the pulpit*
> *To pray for no more.*

Traditionally, the second son entered the army or navy, the third the ministry. As for fourth sons, they often became the adventurers of the family, the *sea uncles* of their siblings' children. From these a good part of Yankeedom's original stock may have come, leaving with us such expressions (now rare) as *free as a fourth son, treated like a fourth son, wild as a fourth son*. Merry rascals, all — and often dying richer than their eldest brothers. But still questionable prospects for marriage.

14. Why would a girl try to *draw first blood*?

For reasons stated above! To draw first blood was to marry the first son of a family.

15. Should you marry *two-sided*?

You durned well better. Two-sided meant that both sides of the marriage came from the same town (or island, where I grew up). The relationships might be rather close, of course, but at least you knew what you were getting. To marry *from away* or *off-island* signified flightiness, dalliance or sheer desperation.

16. What was a *brung-on* bride? A *come-on* groom?

Both were results of *not* marrying two-sided . If the fellow married outside his town or off his island, his bride would forever be brung-on, an unenviable position in a close-knit Yankee community. If, instead, *he* went off to live in her parts, he'd forever be a come-on groom and, if anything, worse off. Many a young couple, so beset, just took off for other parts entirely, Goshening here or there, or maybe heading West.

17. Was a *shiftless* woman lazy?

Shiftless didn't mean lazy in the old days, but without dowry or other benefit — without so much as a shift to her name. Some old tales claimed the bride was married naked, saying her vows through a closet door, as evidence she was bringing nothing to the marriage but herself.

18. Could you have a *Shaker wedding*?

The answer is yes, but a Shaker wedding was no wedding at all: Shakers neither married nor had children (and so have just about died out entire). Shaker wedding was slang for a *consortion* or common-law marriage.

19. How might you *save on the parson*?

Put matters off so long that the parson could do the christening along with the marrying for the same fee.

20. To an old Yankee, what were *women's rights*?

No Yankee worthy of the name *ever* intruded on his wife's (or any woman's) right to cook, bake, wash, sweep, scrub, knit, dust, make beds, beat rugs, or otherwise keep house. Nor would he milk her cow, set foot in her garden, garner her hens' eggs, broom the yard, or split kindling. He knew his proper place and kept to it.

21. In the old days, when did you become a spinster?

Spinsterhood proper took over at thirty, became chronic at thirty-five, terminal at forty. But once that certain misty wistfulness called hope had been conquered, spinsterhood proved to be only a sort of apprenticeship: She got promoted to *maiden lady*. And the maiden lady was not only the very starch and marrow of the Yankee community, but often its heart, mind, hands, and conscience as well. For years, the Yankee schoolmarm was required to be unmarried. Others were the nurses, midwives, *tenders* and mercy-erranders to the old, poor and sick. Their voices (terribly true if truly terrible) led the choir, and no Sunday school prospered without one as a teacher. They were the candy-makers and cookie-dispensers, the stalwarts of the school sociable and the church supper, and — perhaps best blessing of all — they were often the only adults children could call by their first names. All told, no Yankee village could long survive without its maiden ladies.

22. How might you *get the nail* on your spouse?

By burying him or her. Sextons in some places presented the survivor with *the last nail*, left over from the deceased spouse's coffin, that it might be the first nail used on the survivor's. Thus to be *true to the last nail* meant true till death did them part. One widow lady I knew claimed she had six of 'em and was working hard on her seventh. To *get the last nail* also meant to have the last word in an argument.

For Keeping Score

For Keeping Score

For Keeping Score

For Keeping Score

For Keeping Score

For Keeping Score